CHERYL FORBES is a well-known journalist who was for several years an editor and writer with *Christianity Today* magazine. Author of hundreds of articles, she is particularly known for her interviewing skill and her literary criticism. *The Religion of Power* is her first book.

THE RELIGION OF POWER

THE RELIGION
OF POWER

CHERYL FORBES

ZONDERVAN PUBLISHING HOUSE
OF THE ZONDERVAN CORPORATION
GRAND RAPIDS, MICHIGAN

THE RELIGION OF POWER
© 1983 by Cheryl Forbes

LIBRARY OF CONGRESS CATALOGING IN PUBLICATION DATA
Forbes, Cheryl.
    The religion of power.
    1. Christian life—1960– . 2. Control (Psychology) I. Title.
BV4501.2.F5896   1983   241   82-24711
ISBN 0-310-45770-X

Designed by Ann Cherryman
Edited by Judith E. Markham

Printed in the United States of America

83 84 85 86 87 88 / 10 9 8 7 6 5 4 3 2 1

To my editor, Judith Markham,
whose encouragement never flagged.

And to my husband, Allen Emerson,
to whom this book is more important
than it is to me.

CONTENTS

*They had both suffered much among the trum-
pets. . . . And yet he loved power.*
—Anthony Trollope, *The Duke's Children*

PROLOGUE

When I was fourteen, before *Power! How to Get It How to Use It* had been written, before I had ever consciously thought of the question of power, I instinctively practiced much of what that book would contain. In my world—a small provincial high school—I participated in the rituals of power as they existed there and as I understood them. My first power-motivated act does me no credit. I turned my back on my best friend.

Sue and I had been inseparable in junior high. Throughout the summer we had worked together as nurse's aides. But I had decided she was from the wrong crowd, while I desperately wanted to be part of the right one—not an unusual adolescent attitude. So on the first day of school in my freshman year, when my friend entered the auditorium, saw me, and said hello, I deliberately turned my face in the other direction. I refused to speak to her. The girl next to me, thinking I hadn't seen or heard Sue, pointed her out. I said that she and I were no longer friends. I believed she was a political and social hindrance to me, and so did the girl with whom I was sitting. Her response was, "Good."

My behavior was cruel and immoral, yet expedient and successful. I became a member of the right crowd.

By that act, I was guilty of what C.S. Lewis called the sin of inner ringism, what I am calling the worship of power. Lewis believed that power may be *one* of the things a person wants from being in the "inner ring"; I think the desire for power is the cause, the inner ring the effect. I was also guilty of de-facing—dehumanizing or unnaming—another human being. Sue became an unperson to me, and my enemy, though a powerless one. I learned early, through this adolescent incident, that we can do what we want to do, and can gain almost any end, *if* we are willing to pay the price. I hope that I have never again given myself so consciously to the unwritten rituals of power. But I know that I am capable of it.

Since I was fourteen, then, this book has been with me, for it is about power—what it is, what it means, how it seduces and sickens and eventually strangles those who think they control it, but who find in the end that it controls them.

Our look at power will take us to the worlds of Michael Korda and Jane Trahey, will analyze the advice of the self-help books, and will consider the best and worst of secular thinking. We will discuss different means to power and their characteristics—in particular sexual and spiritual, the two means available to and used by many Christians. We will discover that our spiritual uses of the word power, for example, the power of God, the power of prayer, the power of the Holy Spirit, may be more secular than sacred. We will look at key passages of Scripture in the Old and New Testaments to see what the Bible says about power. In reexamining some of our theological assumptions about what true power is, we will learn that our attitudes about leadership, management, and achievement, all of which can be euphemisms for power, may need radical change.

When I looked for books to help me decide what my attitude toward power should be as a business woman and a Christian, I found little help. There are management books for Christians, but for the most part they ignore or side-step the fundamental issue of power. Thus I began to see the need for a book dealing with this subject.

Not that this book is the final answer to the problem power poses: it is not. But it is an initial probe. As you read, put yourself in these situations. If what I have to say has any truth, it may be uncomfortable or downright painful at times. You may not help but see yourself; I am certainly here. But with no one to overhear you, there is no need to pretend or to be dishonest with yourself. You may never have lived every detail of the examples I will cite; however your experiences may be similar. Consider how and why you acted or reacted the way you did. Would you respond differently today?

A book written by Jane Trahey, _On Women & Power,_ affected me deeply and led directly to this one. A former colleague, Mark Bernard, recommended that I read it. The book appalled me as a Christian, a professional, and a woman. It reminded me of the cruel fourteen-year-old I thought I had left behind. I had told myself and others that I disliked office politics. I tried to deal straightforwardly with my colleagues. But I saw myself on too many pages of that book. True, I no longer deliberately and consciously acted as I had years earlier. I did not need to; my behavior had become automatic. Rather than leaving it behind, it had become an intimate part of me.

There I was, but I did not want to remain there. I wanted the work that I felt I was born to do, but I didn't want what seemed to go with it. At a certain point, a Christian must say no to maneuvers and manipulations, to politics and pretendings. The price of power is too high.

Mark Bernard led me to write this book. But it has not turned out the way he intended it to. Even so, I thank him.

1.

1.

THE RELIGION
OF POWER

*This simple fact is that we are all moved without
knowing it by an imperious will to power which
brooks no obstacles.*
                    —Paul Tournier, *The Violence Within*

The "modern idolatry." The necessary ingredient to progress
and economic growth. The fundamental aspect of our nature and
our society. All those phrases can and do apply to power. It is a
god, and a heady, intoxicating one; success is its creed. The
promises of power are hard to resist, and few of us do. What is it
that makes power so appealing a religion—or a religion at all?
And why are Christians as susceptible as non-Christians?

A religion has a set of beliefs, either systematically set forth or
instinctively recognized and accepted by those who hold them.
This set of beliefs includes an element of faith, perhaps a primitive view of cause and effect. And then there are the benefits.
Following certain religious rules will ensure a better, more interesting, more meaningful, and more rewarding life, which is
the implicit promise of any religion. After a lifetime of service,
we may receive recognition by our peers that we are an expert in
the faith. We may be given a measure more of freedom as a
result, or a higher status. We may gain respect, influence, importance, fame, a name—success. Religion always, too, promises some kind of eternal life. It may not be an afterlife; we may

receive everything now. But people will remember us and our accomplishments after we are dead, the way they do Marco Polo or Galileo. There also are implicit threats with the rules. If we refuse to obey them, we risk everything. Now look at power. It also has rules, promised benefits, implied threats. The working out of the rules of power may vary depending on the context, but the nature of the rules remains fairly constant. Power has a dress code, a behavioral code, a language code, a furniture code, a time code. A college professor does not look or sound like an executive or a salesperson, but to succeed he had better not be different from other professors. The same is true for any profession or vocation we could name.

Some people think this results from a herd instinct or from a fear of being out-of-the-ordinary, of losing a sense of belonging or community. That may be part of it. But we could also view it as putting on the garb of a particular order of power.

For example, a tie is a symbol for many professional men. They may not like to wear ties, but they do it. That is a small concession to make. A clean desk is another symbol. Some successful businessmen judge how powerful people are by how bare their desks are. One such Christian businessman, who while alive sat on the boards of many Christian organizations, influenced the appearance of many an office by his clean-desk philosophy. These small matters set the pattern for our behavior in large matters. Unthinking compromises and concessions can lead us directly to power. Not that it is wrong to wear a tie or to work neatly, but if we do so to impress the powerful and to be promoted to that rank we may already be ensnared.

The issue here is symbol—small and great. No symbol is unimportant. Each one marks us, names us, or defines us. The longing to be known and named and understood is one of the deepest human instincts. But that desire may work against us and for the god. Power promises, "I will name you. I will define you. I will tell others who you are. And I will start today." So we begin amassing symbols, clothes, furniture, space, and, finally, people, who are the ultimate symbol. By the time we begin seeing other human beings as symbols, or even as tools who can be useful to us (or our company, or our goals), the god has won.

Just as with other religions, there are recognizable stages in the religion of power. First, the initiation, the stage of the convert, the move from unbeliever to believer. At the outset, we merely listen to what the god will give us in exchange for our worship. Power, though, presents himself differently to each of us, and seldom forthrightly; he doesn't explain the consequences of seemingly harmless initiation requirements. Not many of us can admit even in the privacy of our own closets that we are selfish, prideful, greedy creatures—the weaknesses played on by power.

The second stage, that of novitiate, is not for everyone; many people stop at stage one. Some people may unconsciously join the power novitiate. Even if they don't realize that they have done so, others will. But those who do choose to study more deeply the rituals of the god are on their way to stage three—becoming professionals in the religion, those whose lives are given to the pursuit and study of that religion.

When someone has entered the sanctuary of power and begun walking down its aisles, we know it. It shows in small ways at first, later in larger and larger ways. A person cannot disguise or hide it. The point of power is to be visible, and it promises visibility to the worshiper. A person may become overly concerned about place and space—how large his office is or where it is located. He may ask such questions as: "Is the furniture arranged to make the most of my authority? Is the office arranged to intimidate? Or to make someone so comfortable that he can be caught off guard?" Add to that: title, secretarial help, salary, bonuses, perks, who's invited to what meetings, who knows what and who has the most inside information, who confides in whom, even who plays racquetball (or tennis, or works out—fill in the fad) with whom. Or, who gives in and who is given in to. It doesn't matter how insignificant the symbols are on their own; if someone has enough of them, they gain significance through their number.

Behavior also reveals the seeker after power; how and where a person sits during meetings, whether he arrives on time or late, or bothers to attend at all. Language also informs on him. A person at the altar of power is proud that he can handle people, that he is an expert in office politics. He may brag about his successes and become skillful in telling one person one thing and someone else another. He has told each one what that person wants to hear; he has been tactful and diplomatic. Or so he tells himself.

The people to whom this is done may think they've been manipulated and lied to. They probably have. But the person responsible would never admit he had lied. Two seminary professors didn't speak to each other for years because the dean had told each one that the other was against him. The dean wanted those two men to be enemies, not allies, all for what he saw as the good of the school. Only after the dean left did the professors discover the truth. The dean believed that he was doing God's will and would have been shocked had someone accused him of lying and deceit. He had become a high priest of power.

More than one manager has told me that he loved office politics—the intrigue, the maneuvering—and that he was good at it. These managers manipulated others, tried to divide and conquer staff members, hinted that certain people were not quite as good at their jobs as others thought, whispered promises they never intended to keep. These are the tactics of the secular world. These also, unfortunately, are tactics Christians use.

Although the religion of power is the antithesis of Christianity, Christians participate in it. Some people practice power consciously and willingly, quite often because they believe that power is necessary to promote Christianity throughout the world. Others may practice the rituals of power without consciously admitting that they do. They don't need to; their instincts for the rituals are unerring, like knowing how to breathe.

Whether it is conscious act or unconscious instinct, the reason given is to do God's will or to fulfill a God-given task. At some point the reason may change to something more self-centered, probably will change as power grows, but a Christian who moves into power usually believes that he is justified in doing so. He may believe that he needs power to protect the faith, influence government and political leaders, create an organization or movement to benefit mankind and glorify God. He overlooks, however, the inescapable truth that whoever attempts to wield power will find that power wields him.

The last decade of our history saw many such examples; the Watergate affair is only one example, but one that touched the evangelical community through Billy Graham. Graham sought to influence the president, believing that he had some power over Nixon. Yet he found to his dismay that Nixon had been using him. As Richard V. Pierard said in _The Reformed Journal:_ "The politically naive Graham had learned . . . an important lesson. When one attempts to get close to those who have political and economic power, one runs the risk of being used by the very same person one hopes to influence."

Few people would question Graham's motives in his relationship with Richard Nixon. It is difficult to question _anyone_ who explains that he wants a certain position of authority because God plans to use him in it (which is why this problem is so difficult to deal with). This person may even argue that God has placed him in a position of power for a purpose—and it may be true to a point. Yet the reasoning leaves us theologically uncomfortable. Some Christians describe their success—whether in business, law, or the ministry—in such a way that God becomes, mysteriously, almost superstitiously, the pawn in the game of power whom they use to checkmate their opponent.

Why? Because we never see God in failure, but only in success—a strange attitude for people who have the cross at the center of their faith. We allow only the best-looking, the brightest, the richest, the most sophisticated people into the circle of special Christians.

Power, whether in Christians or non-Christians, operates identically. But to the rituals, Christians, add one more—the language of the spiritual life.

Christians appeal to a person's conscience. They quote Scripture. They use prayer as a means out of awkward situations or uncomfortable confrontations. Resorting to piety is a power play peculiar to Christians. It is manipulation at its worst—and best, since it nearly always succeeds.

This happens in churches as well as in Christian organizations. A choir director came to a well-known suburban evangelical church on the East Coast at a salary larger than the senior minister, whose income was immediately adjusted upward. Whereas the previous choir director had had to struggle for money to buy new music, the new man was given a large budget, a secretary, a full-time organist, and time to compose. Yet his attitude toward other church musicians was that they should "do it for the Lord." What he meant was "for free." That was a power ploy—getting others to feel guilty and not-quite-Christian to gain his own ends.

All of us have at some point in our lives acted this way. We are told in books and magazines and on radio and television that the only way to succeed is to follow the unwritten laws of power. Our government, schools, communities, churches, and even families, can only function through a power structure. We hear this from the pulpit; we see it in action. Nothing can be accomplished without power. Someone must rule; others must submit.

Because all human organizations work through power, we never stop to consider whether *we* ought to participate in it. We have assumed that the fact of its existence is reason enough to acquiesce. Whether you work in a secular or a Christian organization, whatever your profession, if you live and work with people you will at some point confront the rituals of power. Can you recognize them? Should you be able to? Absolutely. As Christians we need to challenge any view that seems so certain of its inevitability, in this case that there is only one way to succeed. We need to understand how power works and admit that this god can control any one of us. We also need to recognize that much of our definition of power comes from secular society, which uses the term in a spiritual context.

No matter how much we claim to follow Scripture, we ignore its demands for a radical life. We don't probe our traditions to see whether they are truly biblical. Our view of power clearly illustrates this: For example, our definition of power does not come from the Prophets, the Gospels, or the letters of Paul. It comes (indirectly) from Michael Korda, Machiavelli, or William Paley. Or from government, from school, from watching people work and maneuver, or from novels. The person who coined the phrase "the corridors of power" was not a politician or chief executive officer but a storyteller, the late C.P. Snow.

The operation of power is the common denominator linking most, if not all, human activity. Even the disciples hungered after the god while in the presence of God. Over and over during the last week of Christ's life the disciples asked who would be first, who was best, or, to put it in modern business terms, who would be Jesus' chief executive officer. Christ was about to suffer an excruciating death—and his closest companions were arguing about power. The arguing continued in the early church—between Paul and Peter, between Paul and Barnabas, between the Jewish and Gentile Christians, among the Corinthian believers. The church has debated the meaning of power ever since.

Today the debate has moved from the church to the business arena. Power affects labor and management. It affects the consumer through monopolies, anti-trust laws, and advertising, to give a few examples. It affects how people work and how they feel about the work they do. Achieving and maintaining power can _become_ one's work.

And this touches the core of the matter. Work is essential. What we do and how we do it can poison or pleasure the other aspects of our lives. Consider this situation. You've been given what may amount to a second sight, an instinctive understanding of your field that could not only carry you to the top but could _by_ carrying you there help you make a first-rate contribution to society. You cannot contribute without authority, and you only receive authority with power. At the beginning you don't ask for the sake of success only, but for the sake of the contribution you believe God has called you to make. Your vision is pure—as much as any human being's can be.

But stop. The dilemma is before you. You see the difficulty. You see that the way to attain authority and the right to make decisions and not merely implement those made by someone above or beside you is to don the vestments of power. Or rather, it is the quickest way. Hard work and ability don't necessarily pay off; other ingredients may be needed. When to flatter. To change sides. To pick the winning team. To cut off a friendship that has become a hindrance. When to keep silent. When to speak the right words or refrain from using the wrong ones. When to argue, when to accept—when to welcome, perhaps—unfair, unjustified criticism. Learning to read between the lines, to sense the hidden agenda, the hidden motives. Suddenly you realize that power may be the very thing that will in the end destroy your contribution. What do you do? Where do you go for help?

Truly a dilemma. For the one thing we must never do is to talk about power. The most powerful men and women deny that they have any power; they don't want people to analyze it. To remain strong, power must remain a mystery.

We cannot escape dealing with power. Either we will be suffering from another person's attempts to gain power, or we will be trying to gain power ourselves. In some way, even though we think that we have rejected the way of power, we may find ourselves involved. We may—at times—think that we will never be able to get on with the job because of the ever-present problem of power.

2.

2.
THE ONLY GAME
IN TOWN

To make the real decisions, one's got to have
the real power.
　　　　　　　—C.P. Snow, *Corridors of Power*

Anyone looking at our society cannot fail to notice our national hunger for power. *Time* magazine uses the word in its advertisements. Lawyers attempt a form of mind control in the courtroom. Psychologists study the power motive of successful managers and disease-prone people. Lobbyists brag about the power they wield. Why this obsession with power?

A business-watcher might answer that the American capitalistic system is undergoing a crisis in leadership; thus the inroads that Japan and Germany have made in the American marketplace, and thus the trade deficit. A government-watcher might say, yes, we suffer from a lack of leadership and an inability to make decisions and stick with them. A church-watcher would ask, where are the young leaders? Religion journalists for the past several years have wondered, where are the young theologians?

Early in our upbringing the longing for power begins. We are raised to take charge of our own futures, to increase intellectually, materially, and emotionally. We want to understand and control our psyches, our families, and our environment, because we feel threatened at every hand.

Primitive man believed himself to be threatened by gods or forces he could not see, and because he could not see them he could not understand them. To these gods he offered tokens of appeasement. "If I and my society do certain things—make certain sacrifices and motions, say specific prayers, perform dances and obeisances—the gods will not harm me. They may even *protect* me from other gods or forces I know even less about," so anthropologists say primitive man may have reasoned.

The difference between such thought and ours today is that the primitives knew they were powerless. We do not. We stamp our feet and declare that it will not be so. We strive to seize control, to protect ourselves from any enemy, whether natural or manmade.

Our government spends billions of dollars developing systems to control our lives. We have controls for weather, for agriculture, for economics, for defense. People have received Nobel prizes for work whose sole purpose is to control, predict, and protect the future.

Look at the defense budget, for example. Every president, no matter how liberal or conservative, vows to maintain a strong defense. Each one declares that military spending is a top priority. Even with the concern over CIA excesses, no one has radically curbed our intelligence force. No one dares; the enemies are too strong and too numerous. If we relinquish our drive for power over our political enemies, they will gain power over us. John F. Kennedy, who loved and understood power, accelerated the space program to prevent the Soviets from gaining the upper hand in outer space. We were shocked and startled to find that they beat us into space. Could they be more powerful than we, we wondered?

Nature, too, is inherently man's enemy, with its whims and excesses—or lack of them. The modern farmer, though still subject to the vagaries of nature, has more power over it than his predecessors who pioneered the land. But our power or control over nature extends farther than controlling pests, drought, floods, or fires. We now have the ability to "remake" nature, as it were, after we have destroyed or depleted it.

If we dirty our air or water, we can reverse the process. If we strip the earth of its nutrients, we can fertilize it. In other words, we can damn and save. Should nature not produce what we want in the quantities we want it, we have learned to approximate its work: margarine for butter, polyester for cotton, plastic or metal for wood, vinyl for leather, synthetic fuels for gas, oil, and coal. Ironically, however, the chemicals with which we clutter our lives also threaten us with cancer and other diseases, with fires that spread more rapidly than those in the past and that burn hotter. The circle is vicious. We invent to protect ourselves, but those inventions in turn bring new threats from which we need further protection. Because we need power to protect us from ourselves, we create a Ralph Nader, who then becomes the power over the powerful.

In economics we see the same principle of power operating. Economists work on systems to predict the future, no more or less than for the same reason that priests and magicians traveled to Delphi or read the entrails of chickens—and often with much the same results. Wassily Leontief, a Russian-born economist who taught at Harvard from 1932-1975, in 1973 received the Nobel Prize for economics. He developed a system for predicting future economic trends, called the input-output system, similar to what France uses. We want a safe economic world and spend billions of dollars hoping to secure it. Will inflation go up or down? What will happen with prices? Or interest rates? No one can listen to the radio, pick up a newspaper, or read a newsmagazine without finding some economic prophet somewhere making predictions.

Our insurance industry, our pension systems, our social security program are all designed to protect us—to give us power over the unknown. The medical field provides some of the most potent examples of this craving after power. The research in eugenics, genetic engineering, and genetic counseling is a case in point. Medical ethicists and philosophers are concerned about fetal research because they believe that it will lead to a segment of society having power to judge which fetuses are worthy of birth and which should be discarded. There is no greater power than the power over life and death. Although we sometimes assume that the Supreme Court's ruling on abortion was the catalyst for the concern, the issues had already surfaced among professionals. A diagnostic technique, amniocentesis, raised some ethical questions. This procedure is used to determine whether there are any chromosomal abnormalities in a fetus. The problem with the technique is what happens after the results are known. Couples who discover that their unborn child may be retarded or have other difficulties have two choices: abortion or carrying the handicapped child to term.

Amniocentesis is the most publicized technique in prenatal testing. There are others: placental aspiration and fetoscopy, newer techniques, are also riskier. The use of prenatal diagnostic testing is in its third decade, and the ethical problems have not lessened. More and more people clamor for mandatory genetic screening and other legal devices to provide man—or a select group of men—with the power to say who can or cannot have children. (HEW under the "National Genetic Disease Act" in 1978 established the National Clearinghouse for Human Genetic Disease.)

Frances Crick, who shares a Nobel Prize with James Watson for discovering the structure for DNA, wants us to decide who should or should not live, and who should or should not bear children. He also believes that a battery of genetic tests should be given infants to decide which ones have been born "legally." I do not raise this to warn people that such an idea is imminently to be adopted. Crick, himself, admits the unlikelihood of this. I merely use it as an example of the pervasive nature of the problem of power.

When we look at the ghettos, we see the opposite problem— people trapped into economic and cultural powerlessness. They are in every way subordinate. Yet, because the desire for power is strong, even within their own powerless society there are power groups and individuals. There are those whose walk indicates that they stand on the power spot, even if that spot is only a street corner or a pool hall. The desire to be known may only be satisfied through graffiti, but it is nevertheless satisfied. In fact, graffiti may be one of the main ways that the powerless reach and in some small sense overpower the powerful. Graffiti is a form of psychological mugging.

Anyone who has ridden the New York subway system knows what I mean. Everywhere you look, an unseen presence assaults you with names, obscenities, or specious philosophy. "Underground art," some patternless and some with a strange structure that has a beauty all its own, never lets a subway rider rest. It is an attempt to control others by fear. Roger Rosenblatt, in a _Time_ essay, commented that graffiti scares people because it is anonymous.

> The "artist" is a sneak thief, and just as he attacks his "canvas" suddenly, his work attacks you. For another, these names (scary in their very loudness) are yelling at you in public places, where you wish to preserve your own name. For a third, there is the terror of the illegible. Most of the graffiti on subways nowadays is indecipherable, which either means that the attack artist is an illiterate—frightening in itself—or that he is using some unknown cuneiform language or the jagged symbols of the mad. And then there is a fourth reason. We have a right to our dullness. We have a right to clean slates, to blank places. Writing on a wall is a way of breaking down the wall. We have a right to some walls.

These pointed comments about this phenomenon of our culture indicate to me that even those who know they are powerless—at least economically—have a way of breaking into power. Our names, and thus our existence and our power, are threatened by the vehemence with which these anonymous names are revealed. As we shall see, a primary promise of power is to give us a name and make it known. In graffiti, the nameless become named. The powerless gain a measure of momentary power.

Everyone has this drive for power. Philosophers Hobbes, Nietzsche, and others, recognized this. In _The Leviathan_ Hobbes wrote:

> So that in the first place, I put for a general inclination of all mankind, a perpetual and restless desire of Power after power, that ceaseth only in Death. And the cause of this, is not always that a man hopes for a more intensive delight, than he has already attained to; or that he cannot be content with a moderate power: but

because he cannot assure the power and means to live well, which he hath present, without the acquisition of more.

In other words, we seek more power for fear that the power we possess will disappear, be lost, or be stolen from us. This is why we meet any attempts to overpower us with resistance.

The advertising industry is impelled by this drive. The small computer industry, for example, shows all sides of the problem. Advertisements appeal to a business person's need for power over his job and his competitor, implying that a particular computer will give him that. Yet companies have found that installing small computers so frightens executives that they refuse to use them. They believe a computer makes them increasingly vulnerable to the power of their boss, who through the computer has unseen access to personal files and records. Managers also fear that they will lose power—control—over the people they are supposed to be managing.

Lest we think that this struggle for power is a human phenomenon only, studies done by sociobiologists show that certain animal societies have definite hierarchical patterns with some groups submissive and others dominant.* These can be simple patterns—one dominant animal and the rest submissive—or more complex with a group dominating the other groups.

Usually the power source is discernible by certain physical characteristics. The leader of a wolf pack, for example, holds his head, ears, and tail in a certain way; he faces other wolves within the pack head-on. Interestingly, he controls the pack with little show of overt hostility. This has also been observed in the dominant male rhesus monkey, who walks slowly and deliberately. Biologists have also discovered that certain animals give acoustical or chemical signals that tell others who is in charge.

Experiments with chickens have shown the fundamental nature of the struggle for power. As soon as a new flock is formed, the fight begins. The more powerful chickens receive more food, have better nests, and gain more mobility, a larger territory in

---

*I am indebted here to information provided by Edward Wilson in his book *Sociobiology.*

which to roam. Dominance in the chicken and other primitive animal societies usually comes through overt aggression.

In a more advanced society, power is maintained by subtler behavior and greater manipulation. There are clear advantages of being dominant: food, shelter, reproduction. But there is also a status in being the power source, a kind of respect or perhaps fear shown to the animal by its associates. The dominant creature usually works less than the others. He doesn't have to struggle for his food, and because he has more of it he and his offspring become more powerful genetically. The stronger animals are also under less stress, for once power is established, they are the least aggressive in a group, thus expending the least energy. (Those on the low end—the most powerless—are nearly as tension free. The males in the middle experience the greatest tension and have the most aggressive tendencies.) Other studies have shown that there are perks for those sitting in the power spot. For example, dominant animals are groomed by their subordinates.

What determines who will dominate among animals? Sex, first and foremost. With certain exceptions (insect societies, for example), males tend to dominate over females. Age is another important factor. Adults dominate the young. Physical characteristics play an important part—strength, quickness, size, or weight. Another interesting phenomenon is that among certain species the mother's rank indicates how far the offspring will travel on the animal road to power.

These instincts have obvious parallels to human behavior. For example, a study of the body language of certain animals could parallel the study of human body language, for the physical characteristics and posturing of powerful people often set them apart. Also, just as certain animals give off an audible or sensory signal, so we recognize certain people as inherently powerful. We may call it their aura, though it may well be their odor. Scientists have determined that people exude an odor—what they call pheromones—something we smell subconsciously and by which we sense kindred spirits, those we dislike, or those who intimidate us.

In animals this power instinct may be a matter of survival. Certainly there is an element of the survival instinct in human beings. But the kind of power we're talking about in humanity takes us many steps beyond pure survival. Although there assuredly have been times in our history when, like the spider monkey, we have slapped and kicked one another, have figuratively roared and ground our teeth at one another, we generally behave in a more understated fashion. We may instead call each other names or try to thwart the efforts of a competitor by outadvertising, by price wars, or by public relations schemes to undermine the other's reputation while at the same time enhancing ours.

We consider this acceptable because it is directed at another organization. Yet this same drive for power can occur *within* an organization. It is common to find the marketing department at odds with research/development. At the root of such intercompany squabbles is usually the matter of who has the power to determine what will be produced, how it will be sold, and, most importantly, how much it will cost and how much the company can spend.

As painful and destructive as a power struggle between divisions is, it is even more wrenching when it happens between individuals within a division. But it happens regularly, and why not? Our longing for power begins early in our upbringing. We are raised to take charge of our futures and to believe that through effort and ability we can gain intellectual and financial power. We deserve to get what we want. Failure is anathema. Boys in particular have this reinforced. They are to be strong, confident, first-place winners. Boys are to conquer their environment, whether it be on the baseball diamond or in the classroom. The demands made on girls, though generally in different areas, are no less stringent.

Last summer at a Little League softball game I watched a father publicly berate his hysterical son, not only for striking out, but for crying about it. The father's disgust and near-hatred were visible on his face for all of us to see, including his son. This man felt powerless because his son wasn't a great player, and the son felt powerless to gain his father's love and respect because he couldn't even make contact with the ball. This is a painful illustration of our refusal to allow failure in our children.

It doesn't take long to convince children and teen-agers that their worth in life depends on their power. Many "computer generation" kids see their power lying in control over equipment. Skill at video games is one form. Computer skill is another. A _Time_ magazine cover story on computer whiz kids quoted a black fourteen-year-old as saying, "I love those machines. I've got all this power at my fingertips." Computers, he added, make him "somebody." And that's the name of the game in town: _power to be somebody._

With this inbred attitude, it is easy to move from video games to a ruthless adult attitude toward getting power. What we don't realize in our rush to win is that once in the game, you can't get out. As long as you are held there, you really are powerless, despite the power you seem to have.

Alexander Solzhenitsyn recognized while in prison that as long as he was trying to maintain some power—whether it was for food, clothing, or health—he was at the mercy of his captors. When he realized and accepted and even embraced his powerlessness, then he became completely free; the power of his captors over him ceased. In the way of life's strange paradoxes, he became the powerful, they the powerless.

We are bred to believe that the proper and natural behavior of human beings is to achieve as much power as we can, to hunger for it. No matter in what circumstances we find ourselves, no matter in what field we earn our living, we seek to control not only the animate, seen, and touchable aspects of our lives, but the inanimate, unseen, and untouchable as well.

Measured next to the ability to grant life or death, a concern with titles, furniture, or space seems petty. But that is probably what most of our power struggles will involve. That, and our ability to have power over people. Ultimately, it is only our ability to make people do what we want them to, for our good, safety, pleasure, or protection, that will assuage our fear of uncertainty, anonymity, namelessness, and death. Power removes our fears—at least temporarily. If we have power, we have a name and a destiny.

3.

3.
NO OTHER WORD

> *It's O.K. to be greedy.*
> *It's O.K. to be ambitious.*
> *It's O.K. to look out for Number One.*
> *It's O.K. to have a good time.*
> *It's O.K. to be Machiavellian (if you can get away with it).*
> *It's O.K. to recognize that honesty is not always the best policy (provided you don't go around saying so).*
> *It's O.K. to be a winner.*
> *And it's always O.K. to be rich.*
> —Michael Korda, *Success!*

No matter where we turn, power faces us. But what exactly is power? Most of us recognize it; we know that certain people have it. But what is it they have? Because power cannot be defined in the *abstract*—at least not easily—we need to explain it through anecdote and case study. How-to authors give one definition of power. Playwrights and novelists set forth a second. Psychoanalysts and sociologists a third.

In the self-help or how-to category, Michael Korda is first among many when it comes to power. His best-sellers on power and success indicate that a lot of people want what he's got. Korda begins his book on power with these words: "The purpose of this book is to show you how to use, recognize and live with power, and to convince you that the world you live in is a challenge and a game, and that a sense of power—*your* power—is the core of it." He ends with: "The more mechanical and complicated our world is, the more we need the simplicity of power to guide us and protect us. It's the one gift that allows us to remain human in an inhuman world—for 'the love of power is the love of ourselves.'" So for Korda, initially power is a game that gives meaning to life. But ultimately it becomes much more than a game. Power becomes our guide and protection, helping us to be human, giving us a name. Those are theological words, and with them Korda has listed the characteristics of a god. In his world, mankind has moved from primitive superstition—from animism and stone idols—through the Judeo-Christian tradition to a religion of success with power as its god. He says we need this guide because our world is too complex.

Between these two extremes—the game and the god—lies Korda's approach to, and definition of, power. One of the first goals is to learn what power is, a discovery that can be made anywhere by anyone (though he admits later in the book that you can't become powerful simply by knowing the rules). But you cannot know it apart from its results. Power must be visible to exist. Whatever techniques bring powerful results are power's tools.

Children learn early what gives them power. Even an infant has this instinct. My niece is consummate at controlling her mother. She puckers her lips, pulls her eyebrows down, wrinkles her forehead, and whimpers slightly—a never-fail means to power in her situation. If she wants admiration or laughter, she uses her face and voice in another way. Older children discover the divide-and-conquer technique of power over their parents (many business managers use this technique brilliantly). What parent hasn't been a part of, and at times a party to, that ploy? Who doesn't remember trying it? If one parent says no, the child asks the other, with the expectation that the second parent will say yes. Parents allow divide and conquer by carelessness or laziness. The "if your mother says it's all right" response promotes the understanding that there are at least two places to go for the answer the child wants. And it's not an answer until the response conforms to the desire of the child asking the question. (This same attitude causes us a great deal of confusion about prayer.) Children also practice power on their peers: "If you don't play by my rules, I'll take my toys and go home." Certain children seem to sense who is vulnerable to flattery or teasing or bribery. They play for power with unerring instincts.

Korda mentions two other techniques children use: withholding affection or vomiting. Obviously, no adult will continue to use the latter to gain power. Yet, sickness is a good way to elicit sympathy or postpone an unwanted task, gain time to solve a problem or avoid it altogether. The idea of withholding affection or approval is more effective in a marital relationship than in a professional one, though it does work in the latter. A good manager should care little about whether or not he is loved, but the desire for approval is so strong that most of us cannot entirely dispense with it.

There are also tricks children learn quickly in school: look busy when you aren't, ingratiate yourself with the teacher, establish a reputation as a winner. A friend of mine in high school—a National Honor Society member—had a system similar to this. During first term, he did his homework and read the assignments. This established in the minds of the teachers the belief that he was an A student. For the rest of the year, he rested on his reputation. It worked. All of us know people whose reputations seem undeserved; they aren't as exceptional as their fame and fortune proclaim them. But these men and women developed their reputations early and have since been reaping the rewards. In the corridors of power, it often is what people think we are, not what we are, that determines success.

There are other small tricks to gaining power. A particularly effective one is to assume the air of power. Hint that you are powerful or are intimate with those in power. Power reproduces itself rapidly. If people think we're powerful, we soon will be. Another clever ploy is to appear to do most of the work, create all the ideas, and be the hub of the wheel when really we are thriving on someone else's abilities. To achieve the same end without nearly the work, we can assume responsibility for a finished job when we actually have done nothing. Many marketing people use this gambit successfully, particularly in a space-ad campaign or direct-mail effort. Advertising people write copy; the art department comes up with a concept; and the marketing people assume the credit. Yet they have done nothing on the project.

Another way to gain credit and power is simply to talk someone else into doing a task for us and then accept the accolades for a job well done. For example, I tell Joe how extremely busy I am and that it would show how much of a team player he is to help out. This plays on Joe's guilt or insecurity. Or I could suggest that he would be doing me a favor. Thus I appear to be granting him power over me. Or, I could tell Joe that I know how much he will enjoy the task, so I'm letting him handle it. I leave his office with the words, "And you can have it completed in a couple of days?" Before he knows it, Joe is doing my job and his. I get the kudos; he gets the work.

Power, that worthy god, once was "thought of as one of mankind's less attractive characteristics, along with violence and aggression, with which it is often confused." Fortunately, says Korda, this is no longer true. Power and its forms have taken on religious, ritualistic significance. Meetings become worship services, business lunches and dinners eucharistic.

People who want to gain power can follow the diagrams and amass the symbols that spell the word. Window offices and impressive furniture speak loudly, but if people don't know how to make the most of them, the symbols won't do them much good. They must make their symbols work for them.

For example, if my window office is in the center of a row of offices, I'd be better off with a windowless office near the person who has the power. And always try to get near a corner office, which is where power resides. (Most of us can name exceptions, I'm sure.) Once I have the right office and furniture, I should arrange the room to give myself plenty of space while limiting the space of any visitors. Long before I had read any books on power I had heard of this technique. A new manager once explained to me that he had placed his desk at a certain distance from the window so as to give himself the spatial edge in any interview. (Why he admitted it to me is still a mystery. Perhaps he thought I was too powerless to worry about, or too naive to understand what he was saying.)

We all know how important it is to amass property to gain power, but only a novice would be satisfied to stop here. A person after power must master a certain way of sitting. He must learn how to attend meetings. Everything he does contributes or hinders his acquisition of power.

If our culture, and thus every aspect of our lives, is motivated for power, we might assume that this is the result of secularism. Not so, say the secularists (like Korda). The American hunger for power lies in our religious history and, specifically, in the Protestant work ethic. The Puritans, among others, believed that people knew one's faithfulness by one's prosperity. The more faithful a person was, the more God would bless him materially, thus giving him wealth, position, and power. As much as we would like to deny this assertion—and it is simplistically overstated—we cannot deny that it has some validity. Protestants have been overly concerned with material possessions and success.

Thus, in quintessentially secular self-help books, we find that definition laid at our feet. Power is a game, which turns into a god, as any game will if played continuously, and we have Protestantism to thank. Rather than the secular influencing the sacred, then, secular thinking is the aftermath of the sacred. As we shall see, the circle is completed when, changed, heightened, or deepened, the sacred incorporates secular thinking back into its being.

However, this worship of the god power, which infects every aspect of our lives today, did not happen without the approval and promotion of secular society. "The religious justification of success," writes Korda, "was now supported by a secular ethic—it was not only one's duty to God to strive for wealth . . . but also a *civic* duty and a duty toward oneself." We see here the difficulty of separating the sacred and the secular, if it can be done, or if it is legitimate to try. Every society contains both, and both constantly ebb and flow into each other.

While this is not a book about political power, but about a struggle for personal power, the implications are clear for the political arena also. Controlling our government, which means our future, is a result of achieving power. We have already seen this in certain fundamentalist and evangelical political movements, whose power-seeking leaders promise increasing activity on a national level in the years to come. Then, they say, we will again be reshaping the secular, as the secular is now reshaping us.

Most of the discussions on power are distinctively male; women have had little or no power, except in their families, where many of the techniques used in business also have been successful. This is changing, however slowly. Books on power for women have come out at an increasing rate in the past few years. Women now offer advice to other women on how to become novitiates in the religion of power—because women have an additional burden as professionals: their sex. Our sex. For even should we decide that we want to walk the corridors of power we may not be able to. The unwritten rituals are still male-dominated. Women are not raised to understand the rules. Women are trained to work alone—in the house, in the kitchen, but never as part of a team. (If you don't think this is true, how many women do you know who can work well together in a kitchen?)

Not understanding the rules is both an advantage and a disadvantage in professional life. Because women don't necessarily understand the rules, they can break them in a way that wouldn't be tolerated by men. Or, women can learn the rules and pretend they haven't, which is even more effective. They can use their sex to enter the inner ring. Men will tell women colleagues things that they would never admit to male colleagues, perhaps assuming that they will not really understand. Women can use passivity, weakness, innocence to get into the circle. We can even use tears. If we are quick and clever, we can also use all the masculine tricks. The sword can become double-edged and swiftly wielded, for with the differences and difficulties there are some striking similarities as well.

Women have an instinct for power that can be exploited successfully, even if they don't understand all the rituals. The essence that powerful people exude, which Jane Trahey calls a perfume, is the goal. Women tell women, "Work for success. Get yourself a network. Break the rules to your advantage. (Since

men think women don't know the rules, they don't expect women
to follow the rules.)

Yet even Trahey defines power in quasi-theological terms. She
says she wanted Ada, the A & P checkout lady, to recognize her.
Only then, Trahey says, would she know she had power. In other
words, a name. Such recognition is a humanizing factor. It speaks about the
deepest need of the human spirit. Power is a game, a mark of
achievement, a religious drive, a civic duty, a quality, a name,
and finally a god to guard, guide, and protect us. It makes the
future sure, the crooked straight, the rough places plain.

Power for intellectuals and businessmen may still be a taboo
subject, but novelists aren't so reticent. They recognize that the
drive for power, which is basic to human nature, ultimately
means power over people. As power is a god who promises us a
name, he is also a god who promises that we will either name, or
deny a name to, others. The god lets us give a little of what he
gives us. Having the trappings of power means nothing unless
they mean everything: power over people.

Novelists are honest and unyielding in their view of life, with
an acute understanding of man's heart. Although there could be
any number of examples of the way novelists treat power, we will
consider only four twentieth-century writers—two British, two
American—C.P. Snow and C.S. Lewis; Ursula K. LeGuin and
John Gardner.

Years before C.P. Snow wrote _Corridors of Power,_ he wrote a
more telling story, a brilliant study of the power-driven mind.
The Masters considers the urge to be not the king, but the
kingmaker, which is the ultimate achievement power offers. The
title refers not only to the profession of the characters, university
fellows, and to the plot, the election of a new college master, but
also to the men who make the master—the masters of their colleagues. Snow's greatest achievement is the interplay between

the characters, the best way of understanding power in any circumstance, real or imaginary.

The power struggle begins as soon as word reaches the faculty
that the current master is near death. Brown, who wants no office
or title but rather hidden power, knows immediately who the
probable candidates will be and which side he intends to be on.
After that, it is a matter of finding enough votes to ensure success. His handling of prickly faculty members is masterly. He
epitomizes the cool, detached diplomat at work, never declaring
his own views, always trying to discover the other fellow's.
Snow shows his insight into a human's hunger for personal power
by giving his protagonist a cause. His motives are noble. Snow
understands that a person must provide himself with a cause to
legitimate his need for power.

Brown shows this as he soothes, flatters, cajoles, prompts, all
with subtle, quiet, unhurried control. Where others would use
space, he uses time. The urgency is there, of course, but in
appearing to stretch time, he gives himself the air of wisdom and
strength. These are the ways of a high priest of power who knows
the rituals as though he invented them.

In every society there are both powerful and powerless people.
Often we know the one by contrast with the other. So here. The
failure of a potentially powerful man underlies the book. Even
men with ability do not always win. Not all novices become full
members of the community. Overconfidence as well as self-doubt
can dissipate someone's potential power. Bad judgment, sloppy
language, or inferior instincts can hasten him out of the gates. For
those committed utterly to the god, the lessons are clear. To gain
everything you must be willing to give up everything, even those
closest to you. Power is an unforgiving taskmaster, allowing no
mistakes.

Although power promises to humanize us, to make us real
people, in reality it dehumanizes us. Power disallows frailty,
misfortune, or relaxation. In *The Masters* the goal ultimately
becomes more than a new master. The goal becomes the souls of
men. In the fray, at least one man is irreparably broken. Powerful
men are made only as others are destroyed.

Fantasy often tells the truth in a way that strikes us more

deeply, because it catches us off guard. We expect "made-upness" in fairy tales; the fantastic details lure us to the truth within the tale. The three remaining writers fall into this category. For Ursula K. LeGuin's _Earthsea Trilogy,_ religion is magic and the wizards, the magicians, are the priests. A name contains the essence of a thing or person. If a person knows someone's name, he can control him. This is also true for the animals or the elements. Only a few people have the gift of being a master namer. (Notice that here, as in Snow, the power brokers are called masters.)

LeGuin's world presents the possibility of ultimate power, of controlling all people and all things. She also shows that power, the meaning behind magic, has spiritual ramifications. In her world, Ged, the protagonist, whose gifts are outmatched only by his will for power, learns something of the true meaning of power. "The truth is that as a man's real power grows and his knowledge widens, . . . the way he can follow grows narrower; until at last he chooses nothing, but does only and wholly what he _must_ do." The way becomes so narrow for Ged that in the end he has only one task—to search for and destroy the evil power he has allowed into the world. But first he must discover its name, which is his own: Ged.

In naming the evil thing with his name, he confesses his worship of the god power. From that moment on he becomes whole. He renounces the misplaced and misguided adoration of power. But before he could renounce it, he needed to learn its true name. So do we. We cannot hide behind euphemisms or platitudes or (even) theology. There is nothing more difficult to do than naming ourselves as the evil one.

Snow presents a view of power that relates to the organizational side of man; LeGuin shows us power as it relates to the spiritual part of his nature. Snow sees power in relationships. LeGuin views it as more mystical, more personal; power exists outside the bounds of reality with a dimension of its own.

For LeGuin, the knowledge of the strength of power comes when we decide _not_ to invoke it. To use another example, in Tolkien's _Lord of the Rings,_ Gandalf warns Frodo not to use the ring of power. The more the ring is used, the stronger it becomes, until the will is destroyed and power—the ring—has consumed the user.

For these writers, power can be a relationship, a state of being, a force, a taskmaster, a threat to true spirituality. It can be acted out in organizations or individuals. Combine the political (organizational) with the individual (spiritual) and you have the church. At least, that is what existed in the Middle Ages through the sixteenth century. Today the combination is found in parachurch organizations, as well as quasi-religious groups. Such a combination breeds organizations other than the church.

John Gardner was intrigued and nearly consumed with theological questions. In *Freddy's Book,* a story within a story, his focus is the church in the sixteenth century, a particularly turbulent time in its history. The Reformation was causing more than theological splits; it was producing new political alignments and social structures, which shows the power of theological ideas. Gardner used the rough texture of this time as the material for a tale that has contemporary applications.

Near the end of the book, a Christian who never listens to the whispers of wickedness, Lars-Goren, discusses the new religion, Lutheranism, with Bishop Brask, a man who wants power for good but finds himself corrupted in the process. Brask believes the new religion to be in many ways simply another word for power. Lars believes that the use of power is acceptable provided that the motivation is right. The Bishop, a man of experience, knows this is not possible. He asks Lars-Goren a telling question:

> What of the well-meaning and canny political manipulator, a man like Gustav Vasa in his early days—the man who communicates truth, or so he'd claim, by simplification: complicated truth reduced to slogans? How in heaven's name do we communicate with him, or with those he has taught to use his methods? There's the future, I think, power bloc against power bloc, lie against lie, until finally no one knows anymore that he's lying; fact and that-which-seems-desirable-in-the-long-run becomes hopelessly confused, and the man who tells the truth, that is, sticks to the plain facts, is dismissed as a lunatic, or troublemaker, an enemy of the good.

Isn't that how we feel about our government and its leaders? Isn't that how many of us feel about the organizations with which we do business? Do we ever believe that they tell us the truth? Or what about those people in an office who refuse to participate in any power bloc? They are, indeed, called troublemakers. Such people interrupt the rituals; they point to what they are, an intolerable situation to those in charge. The house of cards collapses with just a whisper of the truth.

But to completely understand what Gardner is telling us about power, we need to look at Freddy, the character who is author of *King Gustav and the Devil,* the book within the book. Freddy is a monster, a giant by some genetic fluke. Size frightens people, and so Freddy has always frightened his teachers and classmates. Size also symbolizes power, and Freddy has the power to cow others. Freddy is potentially powerful or powerless. He is a freak of nature, a weak, handicapped person, part of the dispossessed. Yet he also knows, and in some sense fears, the power within himself. So he locks himself in his room to read and write. The only person he sees is his father. His brilliant mind may be as large as his body, but this too he hides; no one has yet seen his book, not even his father.

Freddy chooses to renounce power for peace. When his serenity is threatened, he retreats more deeply and completely. Yet this renouncer of power has written a story of power at work. No one understands power better than someone who has none and who knows, as Freddy does, that to look for it would mean destruction.

Gardner adds another element to our definition of power. He dwells on the darker side of power from the perspective of the powerless. Each of us has the potential for power in some area; at the same time, each of us is powerless. There is always someone stronger, quicker, and better than we are. Gardner shows us power by its contrast. In a way, he and LeGuin come to the same conclusion: power, because of what it is, cannot be used. Ged, though, adds the proviso that power may be invoked in dire need. Freddy, perhaps because of his size and the potential physical harm he could do if provoked, believes there is never a motive pure enough or a need urgent enough to resort to power. Better to admit his powerlessness and live apart from humankind. As long as there is no personal relationship, there is no danger from power. Paradoxically, as Freddy strives to remove the threats of power, he finds power controlling his ability to move about in the world. Power ultimately paralyzes, no matter what its form or function.

In *Till We Have Faces,* C.S. Lewis shows us how powerlessness transformed into power can devour everything in its path, not deliberately or consciously, but thoughtlessly, almost naturally. This, too, is a book about relationships: familial, tutorial, ruler to subject, man to God. Shot through each relationship is the presence of power—ultimately the power over God or the gods, the power to face them legitimately as an equal. What naming is to LeGuin's world, having a face is to Lewis's. And as Gardner's story was told from a posture of powerlessness, so, too, is Lewis's.

In the ancient time of the story's setting, there was no one more powerless than a woman. Yet this is a tale told by a woman about a woman—a woman at war with her family, her teachers, her culture, her religion, and herself. Her name is Orual, and she is heir and eventual queen of a small, superstitious, backward, powerless country; she is also ugly. In that land an ugly woman, even though a potential queen, has no resources for power. At least, not on the surface. But Orual learns to use her unloveliness as a weapon for power to gain the love and the appearance she craves. Power promises her love; power promises her a face. Orual also learns that love is power; for one as unlovely as herself it can be the greatest of all means to power. Anyone who has struggled to develop and maintain close relationships will recognize her techniques.

Orual tries to gain a face with her power. When she finally realizes that her attempt has been a self-serving search for proof that she is loved, God offers her the opportunity to repent and renounce power. He offers her a face. God gives Orual what power only promises.

Each of these novelists does much more than talk about power.

No great work of fiction can ever be summed up so simply, and I don't want to leave the impression that Snow, LeGuin, Gardner, or Lewis can be so easily reduced. But that is not to deny that one of their main themes is power—what it is, how it operates, what it costs.

Lewis presents the most personal picture of power, which is based on a need for love and acceptance. People who love greatly, or whose sense of loyalty and duty toward another is strong, will almost joyfully sacrifice themselves to power. We may submit to a manager, a company, a spouse, or a mentor; in doing so, we allow ourselves to be powerless. Yet as I said, everyone at some point is both powerful and powerless. It is crucial in certain situations to know which we are.

The self-help books teach us that power is a necessity, a guide, a protector. These novelists show another aspect of power. In seeking for a definition of power, we find, paradoxically, that power _is_ definition. Call it definer, namegiver, or face-maker, say the storytellers. By saying that they have explained that power appeals to the deepest need of human beings, which is what makes its danger so strong.

How-to books now seem to be yielding to more serious studies of those who serve power. These works interview, analyze, and categorize people into personality types; their context, generally, is the American corporation.

Michael Maccoby is one such analyst. Of the personalities who play for power, he delineates the most interesting as the jungle fighter (subdivided into lion and fox) and the gamesman. In my experience, most power players fall into one of these two categories.

The goal of the jungle fighter is power over people. Without that, he cannot wholeheartedly believe the image he has created. Quite often such a person also needs to be seen as doing some good work. He seeks to control others because he knows what is best for people. His motives are righteous, not wicked. He poses as philanthropist or benevolent dictator. (Many entrepreneurs, such as Andrew Carnegie, are jungle fighters.) Making money really isn't the issue, though such a person does make money along the way. It is, as David Halberstam said of Henry Luce, what money will do, rather than the money itself that is important.

Henry Luce was just such a jungle fighter. Born in China to missionary parents, he never lost the missionary zeal that moved them, though his cause was to make American political life what he thought it ought to be. He wanted his country governed according to his views. Halberstam says of Luce: "Power, not money, fascinated and moved him." (Originally Luce planned to name *Fortune* magazine *Power*.)

In Luce's zeal to reform America, he manipulated people and the news to present what he thought the public should know. He did this with Theodore H. White and China; he did it later with Vietnam. Luce set up an editorial process that prevented correspondents, as well as most of the editors, from operating from a position of power. The writers had no say in what went into the magazine. They filed copy and the editor(s) rewrote it. The system still exists in great part today. Luce embodied Maccoby's jungle fighter, both lion and fox, in one man.

Lions like to dominate, says Maccoby, "through their superior ideas, courage, and strength; others follow them because they are feared and revered, and they may reward the loyalty of worshipful subordinates." Such people want to be seen as kings, in the historical sense of that word: always right, always brilliant, always surrounded by cheering courtiers, ruling by divine ordinance. Some such leaders will even introduce themselves as kings when asked what their position is. (An example: "This is Steve Steele, Mr. White." "And what do you do here?" responds White, innocently. "I'm the king," explains Steele. This is a true anecdote, but the names are changed.)

Some lions dominate with their joking manner. They intend others to recognize their power through the offbeat way they speak of themselves. Some dominate through size. A Christian businessman, who is about 6'8" tall, never lets you forget his size. At every meeting, at every luncheon, whether social or professional, he refers to his size. This person never intends anyone to take his size for granted. He understands too well what a weapon of power it is.

Short men, heavyset men, or thin men also can, and do, play on their physical characteristics. Women, of course, are not immune to this ploy; using femaleness can be one of the most effective means of getting power. (The combination of sexuality and brains is difficult to ignore. We will consider this at length later.) Whatever stratagem is used, the purpose is to keep others off-balance and out of control. The purpose is to be the only one who is fully in charge.

On the other hand, foxes act just as the name suggests: subtle, sneaky, crafty, manipulative. A fox will promise great things in order to seduce you, only to betray you. He is a Don Juan character who receives sexual gratification from the power techniques he uses and the results gained thereby. In effect, he rapes women and emasculates men. "Give me everything you have, and I promise to reward you. I swear I'll respect you in the morning." He might offer money or advancement. Or your _own_ empire, where you can do to others as he has done to you. (Some companies actually look for people they call "empire-builders.") But once you give the fox—or the company—everything, your usefulness will end. You will be destroyed.

These Don Juans are destructive, immoral creatures who violate the nature of God's highest creation, humankind. They view others as toys or tools to be played with and used. In the end, of course, such behavior will only destroy those who practice it. We cannot treat others that way without receiving the same treatment from someone more powerful. We cannot dehumanize others without at the same time dehumanizing ourselves. Despite what we may be told by company executives or management theorists, this is not an economic battle, or a battle for profits against losses, or successes against failure. This is a battle for the soul.

In the process of dehumanizing everyone around him, this jungle fighter has only two options: kill or be killed. There is no thought of coexisting with wild animals or unfriendly elements; it simply cannot be done. Yet even in winning, such a person loses. He must always be alert for danger. Because there are threats to his power everywhere, he can never relax and enjoy what he's worked for. He trusts no one and has few, if any, satisfying personal relationships. He has only the god power to cling to, and even that could leave him at any moment. In short, this person judges everyone according to his own actions and reactions; and because he has treated people as less than the creatures God intended, he ends up—unintentionally, you may be sure—treating himself the same way. Eventually, he becomes his own victim. In luring recruits and worshipers, however, the god power never reveals the consequences of service. The footnote on his recruiting poster is in invisible ink, not fine print.

The other risk the jungle fighter runs is that his tactics may fail, despite his best efforts. People will only tolerate being treated as tools for so long. Depending on the personalities and goals of those around him, his fall might come quickly. Intellectuals or people with imagination or strong intuitive gifts will not long be cajoled into serving the jungle fighter, who will be left drained and weaponless in his own jungle.

In Maccoby's view, the jungle fighter is not a good leader. But the gamesman is not much better. The gamesman's goal is to win, in contrast to the goal of the jungle fighter, which is power over people. Yet, we must assume that to win means to gain power. Although the gamesman may use different techniques, or better disguise his true desires, if winning is the only thing that counts with him, then power, too, is the only thing that counts. The gamesman wants influence, which only comes with power, and sees all human relationships as a game. This, too, de-humanizes the player and the pawns.

The conclusion, then, is that power reflects personality. Because of certain patterns established as a child, a person grows up with a need to be powerful; his identity is incomplete without it. He needs to have others fear him; their insecurity gives him security. Life is a series of athletic encounters, each one more demanding than the last, with the gold medal of power as the reward.

For Abraham Zaleznik and Manfred F.R. Kets DeVries, power is "what makes people tick, organizations run and executives manage" (the subtitle to their book, _Power and the Corporate Mind_). In other words, power, the measure of success, is an addiction. Powerful people are driven by a need for identity. Imposing power on another individual brings not only a feeling of control, but of omnipotence. When a power-driven person is denied power, he may become angry or hurt, his behavior erratic and irrational. If that person is a manager, his employees may find themselves constantly off-balance.

A power-seeking professional may be trying to compensate or overcompensate for a lack he feels within himself. Someone who secretly believes himself to be unqualified for the job may wield a heavier hand than someone who is confident. Or he may want power to show himself and others that he is as good as he says he is. Perhaps his drive for power stems from the prodding of others—superiors, spouse, parents. He may be making up for some other lack—physical size, presence, voice, looks. Someone at some time may have predicted that he would fail; every notch up the ladder means that he has proven that person wrong. A person's drive for power may even be a substitute for what he really wanted to do but couldn't due to lack of talent, opportunity, or encouragement. Or he simply may want power so much that he wills any sacrifice.

Power metaphorically waves wands over other people. It opens doors without any abracadabras. It demands homage, awe, even fear. Nothing so affects our attitudes toward others as power. Every one of us recognizes the uniqueness of someone who has it—whether we like the person or not. The siren-like quality of power is evidenced by the very success of "how-to" books on power. Powerless people want to know the magic formula for becoming powerful. Every ugly duckling wants to become the beautiful swan. John Doe wants to become Horatio Alger. They believe these books will tell them how to do it. The authors get wealthy (more powerful) and the rest can pretend that power is right around our corner.

People who have no power individually may have it collectively, according to Elizabeth Janeway in _Powers of the Weak_.

She also recognizes the religious nature of power and draws a parallel between power and magic. All religion includes an aspect of "magic." In the past, uneducated, weak people needed to know there was some being greater than themselves who controlled the universe, who had power. Since these people knew they couldn't control their lives, their sanity required belief in a pantheon of omnipotent beings. Now, says Janeway, we no longer need this belief. We need just the opposite. We need to know for sanity's sake that *we* can control our lives. As LeGuin says, in seeking the power to control, we become the god.

Many psychoanalysts believe that mental illness springs from a kind of powerlessness, an anguish that there is no hope, no power to control behavior. Some people are so overwhelmed by the hideous in life that they become powerless to act; despair overtakes them. The irrationality of life—which most of us at one time or another have faced—is more than some people can accept. One person meets it with rigid laws, patterns, or structures. That is a way to power. Another fights it by living chaotically.

Sociologists and psychoanalysts, then, see the desire for power as the result of a deep-seated problem or need. It is an expression of a personality who may be compensating for or reflecting his upbringing, who may be struggling to "be" somebody or trying to prevent himself from feeling obliterated. Power may return a sense of the supernatural to a life that is separated from any reality beyond the senses. Thus the need for the rituals, vestments, and signs, the participation in a form of religion. Power may also, to use another image, become a club where the members recognize each other by some external feature (Brooks Brothers' suits, hand-sewn loafers, maleness, whatever the uniform might be). It brings an I-am-not-alone feeling. Better still, since the power club may be small and very exclusive, it brings a feeling of importance, of being inside, of being part of a special group of people whom others recognize as powerful.

These are, with the exception of C.S. Lewis, the secularists. Their definitions of power may be those that Christians would reject—or say they reject. Yet, many of these books are recommended reading by Christians who write or lead seminars on management.

Is our view of power more secular than we would like to admit? Is it any different from that of Korda or Snow when we are on the Lord's side?

4.

4.
WHAT PRICE POWER?

Instead of truly knowing God as our divine parent and serving him by taking responsibility for each other as brothers and sisters, we use God and others for our own purposes.
—Richard Quebedeaux, *By What Authority?*

With all the anguish about creeping secularism, with all the anxiety about loss of values in our public school system and in our government, it would seem logical to conclude that Christians would be speaking out vigorously against the infiltration of power into our vocabulary, our methods, our goals, and our lives. Unfortunately, this is not happening. If you strain, occasionally you can hear a voice or two rising to order. Wait a minute, these voices say, is this what it's all supposed to be about? But for the most part these voices come from without mainstream evangelicalism and so are shouted down, if they are noticed at all. Henri Nouwen or Richard Foster do not disturb conservative Christianity. With the exception of Nouwen, the voices seldom even phrase their questions to include the word "power," though that is at the heart of their concern. Perhaps it is easier to disregard the voices when they use words like "authority" or "simplicity," which do not carry the impact of the question, "Is it right to angle for power?" For that is the question.

If the secular world is motivated by the quest for power, can we also be motivated in the same way and still claim to be different? We profess that lust, or greed, or selfishness are sinful and should not sway us. Yet these are mere symptoms of a desire for power. Our behavior indicates that we are indeed motivated by power, and thus by lust and greed and selfishness. So a more basic question might be, "Do we, by calling power by other names, by euphemisms, conveniently deny our motivations?"

What are these euphemisms? One of the most widely used is *success.* We simply will not settle for anything less than success. The only way we know God loves us is by the success we achieve. In fact, we would hardly believe that we *were* Christians if we weren't successful. Non-Christians write books to help other non-Christians achieve "power." Such blatancy offends us, so we hide behind the word success, or, perhaps, achievement. Christian publishers offer us books that help us learn how to succeed; and we buy them, by the hundreds of thousands. If it worked for someone else, we know it will work for us.

We don't have to read very far to figure out exactly what these books are teaching. Let's look at two examples: *How to Make a Habit of Succeeding* (the cover says "more than 225,000 in print!") and *Success Can Be Yours: How to Cultivate the Habit of Succeeding* (70,000 copies in print!). Mack R. Douglas, author of both books, tells us that we can succeed by "power of purpose"—"finding, developing, and understanding the purposeful goals that will bring you the achievements you most desire." In the interesting foreword to *How to Make a Habit of Succeeding,* by W. Heartsill Wilson, we learn that "success is not made for the masses, but rather for that select few. . . ." So, for all those masses who bought this mass market paperback and don't succeed . . . you can't say the book didn't warn you. This book combines the worst of all the appeals to power: it guarantees power and at the same time withdraws the guarantee. Douglas plays to the reader's innate desire to be somebody special. "Anybody can have power; well, not just anybody; I mean, you have to be a somebody to really have power," to paraphrase his argument. The basic appeal of power—to think yourself different and better than your fellows—is the motivation here in black and white.

We would like to believe that these books approach success

differently than the techniques used by secular people (remember, Korda's sequel to _Power_ was _Success_). Unfortunately, they don't. The recommendations are to think big, act aggressively, never say no, dress correctly, imagine yourself successful, court fame, fortune, and success, and above all have a "burning desire." "Burning desire is power." Douglas stresses that the success-oriented must compete, maintain the right mental attitude, and practice positive thinking.

This attitude (meaning, all of the above) is legitimized by a spiritual caveat, the kind of tip of the hat to God that the Israelites were guilty of and that the Old Testament prophets deplored. In fact, these books (and numbers like them) promote success as not only part of Christianity, but the very heart of what God wants for his people. And what does author Douglas recommend we read for further enlightenment? A sampling: _How I Multiplied My Income and Happiness in Selling; You Can Change Your Life Through Psychic Power; How I Discovered the Secret of Success in the Bible; The Magic Power of Self-Image Psychology; The Power of Your Subconscious Mind; Success Through the Magic of Personal Power._ Remember LeGuin's view of power as magic? She may write it as fantasy, but Christians are buying it as truth.

Where did we ever get the idea that the Bible holds the key to success? How did we decide that Christianity "does" something for us? By our words and deeds, we proclaim that the only reason Christ came was to _give_ us things—and we don't really mean eternal life but the life that is eternally pleasurable here and now. Somehow we have forgotten that Christ said his peace is not like the world's. However, if it's not like the world's, we don't really want it.

Other euphemisms we use employ the very word "power." Our vocabulary is sprinkled with them. We talk of the _power of possibility thinking_, the _power of positive thinking_, the _power of the Holy Spirit_, the _power of the blood_, God's _power to heal_, and so forth. But what do we mean when we say these things? We mean that with a token nod to God we can think and act our way into what we want. If we want big churches, we can do it. We've got the power. Do we want money? Right. No problem. Just follow these steps. We act as if God gave us a money-back guarantee with his command that we pray for our daily bread. If we don't approve of abortion, or busing, or decreased defense spending, we've got the power to make changes. We've watched the methods of "the world"; we're sophisticated. We use any resource or technology to gain our ends. All that power is at our disposal; it is our "God-given mandate" to use it.

God has become our Permissive Parent. We would never promote such a view of parents in our human families. Permissiveness is one of the evils of our secular society. Except when it comes to ourselves. Then we expect God to "do great things for us"—to give us what we want. That's how we prove he exists.

Which leads us to the ultimate euphemism—the power of *our witness*. We convince a secular world to accept our god by sharing our witness—by showing them what God has given us, whether it's pink Cadillacs, the American way, or crystal cathedrals. Otherwise, who would trade fame and fortune for the agony of self-sacrifice, of commitment, of caring more for others and God than we do for ourselves? Our witness won't work if we show how hard it is to be a Christian. We don't want to admit that Christ died on a hard cross for an ugly mankind.

We like knowing that famous and beautiful people are Christians; it makes us average Christians seem that much more important. But the ugly, the maimed, the poor, the weak, the untalented? What about the God Man in whom there was no beauty? Jesus had no influence, riches, power. He was in human terms a loser. No, we can't project that image: And image is all. Who would buy our product without the right packaging? Would we have bought it in the first place? Unless Christianity works, what good is it?

At the same time that we have trivialized God's role we have made God our friend, Jesus our good buddy. That mental leap is possible because God is there to give us what we want, to help us out, to buck us up. Isn't that what friends are for? But all the while, though we say "Jesus and I are friends," we're subconsciously thinking, "I am in charge of this friendship." It is nearly impossible to have a truly egalitarian relationship with anyone, at least most of the time. Sometimes one person is in charge, sometimes the other. This is as true in marriage as in other relationships. But when it comes to our relationship with God, we almost always act as if we control him. We move him; he doesn't move us. Our lips may say this is not so, but our lives belie our lips. We have our hand on him, not vice versa.

While the books cited earlier may be extreme examples of the kind of thinking that parades itself as abundant Christianity, there are other more subtle and thus more dangerous books that pander and promote the idea that failure is un-Christian. Many of these are books on management, leadership, motivation, or family life; yet they promise more than they can possibly deliver. For people who don't read, there are leadership seminars that teach techniques of manipulation and mind control (over yourself and others). The visibility of media preachers compounds the problem.

In *By What Authority?* Richard Quebedeaux traces how "New Thought"—originally the basis for such cults as Christian Science—and evangelicalism fused in the beliefs of Norman Vincent Peale and Robert Schuller. Much of what is said as if from God is no more than a Christianized version of *est* or some other cult. We would never think of sending money to the Moonies, but we will contribute to those who essentially preach the same thing. As Quebedeaux puts it, success is the "preeminent value," the point of all our religion. What Quebedeaux overlooks is why we want success.

We want success because it gives us power.

In this new interpretation of Christianity, God is no longer our Creator and our Judge. No, he is our ultimate weapon in a lifelong game of power. When we pray—for we believe in the "power" of prayer—we are moving God so that we can defeat our opponent. As Quebedeaux repeats throughout his book, we use God. If he isn't ultilitarian, if he doesn't provide what we want, then he simply isn't there. Certainly we behave as if that were the case, despite all our protestations that God's power enables us to have and do all these things.

Even theologians are infected by the influence of these Christian powerbrokers. When *Christianity Today* decided to begin a new magazine for ministers, the publishers decided to call it *Leadership,* a significant name. Ministers want to think of themselves as "leaders," as the people in charge, the bosses, those to whom the rest of the Christian community look up. The advertisements for *Leadership* appeal to this desire to be "somebody."

It is also significant to note the theme for the first issue: "Power and Authority." In introducing it, the publishers ask, "Who does run the church? Who should have the authority and power? *Leadership* research confirms that 'fuzzy' conceptions of authority and power are the seedbed for major conflicts within the church." The peculiar thing about this issue is that rather than questioning what power is and whether Christian ministers ought to strive for it, the editors assume that power is something that ministers *must* have. They try to give political advice as to how to make it happen. They discuss who has the power—the people with the money—and why they have the power—because they have the money. But, to help the minister see that he can circumvent all that and still get what he wants, we read that "a pastor, then, has not only the authority base but a major power position through his preaching." That is, he can claim that God has put him there.

The minister, of course, is the God expert in the church; that's what he gets paid for. He has power because he is visible. He preaches from the pulpit. This advice and comfort is for the local pastor who may not be well-known, but whose "authority" comes from much the same position as a well-known preacher —from being a God expert. Television preachers are highly visible; they look successful. A local minister can look equally successful in his own context.

The first issue of *Leadership* may offer pragmatic help for the minister to maneuver and manipulate his way into control, but it offers little theological guidance as to the nature and role of a true leader. Jesus Christ the servant leader cannot be found. So, even our supposed theological writers judge Christianity by how well it works, which means, how well it provides us with what we want. Self, not servant, is at the center.

The same thing seems to be happening within the Christian women's movement. Patricia Ward and Martha Stout in their otherwise superb book *Christian Women at Work* recommend that women develop the same kinds of networks and techniques for advancement that men have always had. Although they reject the kind of blatant behavior Betty Lehan Harragan advises in *Games Mother Never Taught You,* they nevertheless believe that power is something a Christian woman must use in order to move ahead in the world of careers. "Using power to effect change," they conclude, "can be a calling that is as valid as the voluntary renunciation of power which Jesus modeled."

Ward and Stout recognize, however, the risky nature of what they recommend. They also say that our culture has confused the nature of power and responsibility by "personalizing" power.

But this is always what happens with power. Power promises to personalize itself in us. It incarnates itself through us, and does so by taking us over. Therefore, if using power is so risky, so fraught with the possibility of driving out the Spirit, ought Christians to gamble, no matter how good the reason?

Richard Foster is a new theological voice, whose first book *Celebration of Discipline* brought him to the attention of the Christian reading public. His second book, a detailed look at one of the spiritual disciplines, simplicity, is uncomfortable reading and contrary to this new virtue of Christianized power. His advice will not win him mass approval. He doesn't promise things; he has no simple formula for success. In fact, his definition of success might look very much like old-fashioned failure, if judged by human eyes. "Turn your back on all high pressure competitive situations that make climbing the ladder the central focus," he writes.

The fruit of the Spirit is not push, drive, climb, grasp, and trample. Don't let the rat-racing world keep you on its treadmill. There is a legitimate place for blood, sweat, and tears; but it should have its roots in the call of God, not in the desire to get ahead. Life is more than a climb to the top of the heap.

But push, drive, climb, and compete are the verbs that govern our lives. While we are pushing, driving, climbing, and competing our way to power, we have no time to sit still and know God.

This pushing and driving can come in the form of sophisticated publicity techniques, the kind Falwell and the Moral Majority use: grass-roots support, sophisticated telephone and direct mail operations, language that "pushes the right buttons"—that phrase meaning "it'll sell." Money affects how much power we have in our society, so such groups strive for it. Visibility is also important, so they keep themselves visible. Schuller is a prime example of this with the Crystal Cathedral. When *The New Yorker* did a story on architect Philip Johnson, the first third of the article was about Schuller and his church, which Johnson designed.

Many Christians today want to make Christianity popular. We want to see Christianity in a physical way. Here we've been influenced by science; nothing is real unless we can see it, feel it, hear it, taste it, touch it, smell it, or spend it. It has no value otherwise. The corollary, of course, is that the greater the visibility, the greater the worth. We are so busy trying to spend our Christianity that we've forgotten the whole point—to spend ourselves.

That's what has happened to us with power. We are so concerned to show the world what a good life Christians have, and thus prove to them that they should join up, that we have decided that the end *absolutely* justifies the means. And the means is power. Christian organizations spend a lot of money, time, talent, imagination, and energy each year for power. We may call it witnessing, we may call it influence, we may call it using modern technology for Christ's sake. That veneer is certainly present. A scratch will show the veneer for what it is.

It's easy to see this among some evangelical leaders today. The examples are well-known and have been discussed in books before Quebedeaux's was published, and will be again. He points out that each leader is building a monument, a permanent structure of some kind, to ensure that his influence and power will not die with his body. Robertson and Bakker are building schools. Oral Roberts has a hospital—and whose praying hands are those sculpted in bronze in front of the hospital? Schuller has completed his Crystal Cathedral. The Billy Graham Center has been opened. Has any other century or any other country seen so many Christian structures named after its Christian leaders?

Foster pinpoints an area where we can definitely see our use of modern techniques in "empire-building"—the direct mail letter begging for money. "It is one thing to inform people of legitimate needs," he says.

> It is quite another to purposely calculate emergency appeals so as to gain the largest response. It is one thing to teach about the spiritual necessity of giving; it is quite another to make use of psychological techniques that are proven to increase giving but have no regard whatsoever for the spiritual state of the individual. It is one thing to help people understand their responsibility for justice and evangelism; it is quite another to persuade and cajole and manipulate the emotions.

He goes on to say that he no longer reads appeals for money that employ the right direct mail techniques—the underlining in red or blue (though red has been proven the most effective color), or the pseudo-handwritten note enclosed with the typewritten letter. But these things work, someone may protest. Perhaps. But as Foster points out, conviction is the work of the Holy Spirit, not ours. Again we have taken over the reins of power from God.

These are not petty issues. Our relationship to God and to power, to means and ends, to image and reality, matter deeply. Has this business of power, whether it be for the business of conversion or as an aid to the hungry or Christian education, this effort to gain power for the sake of the kingdom numbed us so that we cannot "ask the moral questions" (as Foster puts it in another context)? Do we no longer know what morality is? Do we no longer sense that it is better to fail than to succeed, because the price of power is too high?

5.

5.
POWER THROUGH SEX

Keep them barefoot, hungry, and pregnant.

Keep them barefoot, hungry, and pregnant.'' That simple, declarative sentence is a philosophy of power. Sexuality is one of the oldest means to power. Kings, and the occasional queen, have used it, as have the common husband and wife. It operates in businesses and schools, wherever people intermingle. Of all the means to power—intellectual, financial, psychological—it is the most basic. Everyone practices it, Christian and non-Christian alike. No matter how much we want to avoid it, we cannot talk about power without talking about sex.

Where you have two people in some kind of community, you usually have a power struggle. This is true in marriage as well as in other kinds of community. Until recently within our culture the person to gain power in marriage has been the male. Leaving aside the theological considerations of why this has happened in Christian marriage, look at how it's been accomplished. The pattern begins before marriage. The man holds the means to power. He makes the first move. *He* decides where to go on a date, whom to ask, and when (obviously, I am speaking of Western culture as we have known it for the past two hundred years or so). *He* decides how much money to spend. And *he* decides whom to marry—the ultimate power in the male/female relationship.

Traditionally, then, the woman waited while the man operated. And if the woman lived in a culture that demanded she marry or be thought ugly, unpleasant, or a failure, she took anyone who asked. She wanted children, he wanted a housekeeper and bed partner; the pattern of power was determined. The woman had made a bargain. If later she decided it was a bad one, it was too late. The children needed her. The hours were filled with the ordinary, and somehow comforting, tasks of cooking, cleaning, washing, and ironing, which drugged her until she was unable to think about her powerless state. She was raised to be what her mother and grandmother were before her.

The husband, too, may have had an inkling of the bad bargain, but he at least left the house every day to conquer new worlds—play for more power—if only in an innocent flirtation with the new secretary, or in ordering about the old one, who, just as with his wife, had to do what he said because it was her job to obey and his to rule.

Then, because the husband was the breadwinner, he could keep his wife submissive by keeping her just a little hungry, never quite satisfied. Or he could make sure she was always slightly off-balance with not quite enough spending money or uncertain when he would demand to see the checkbook or the accounts.

Hungry, yes. Barefoot? Perhaps not quite, but who decided when she got new shoes? Food? Shelter? Who paid for them? Of course, the ultimate stroke in keeping a woman dependent was pregnancy, and dependency was a goal of power: to have someone, or several people, totally dependent on you, vulnerable, and at your mercy.

This is not meant to be a hostile look at a still-too-common stituation, but rather an honest one. I don't think I exaggerate. Many Christians behave this way out of theological convictions. However, some of us use this as an excuse to behave secularly, to align ourselves with the god power.

Men have used their sexuality as a means to power in a very

simple way (so have women, as we will see later). Because of their gender, they have felt that they deserve the power. This cultural phenomenon is slowly changing and for one reason— because women don't need men the way they once did. Women are educated and working. Even married women are no longer subject to the subtle and not-so-subtle power pressures of their husbands. A woman no longer waits for a man to ask. She can take the initiative. She earns money, buys her own clothes and food, provides her own shelter. She need not have children if she doesn't want them. This removes a basic sexual means to power from men's hands, so now we are told that men are threatened. Some sociologists and psychologists even claim that men are emasculated by the new woman (and thus the rise of homosexuality). This reverses the wicked seductress syndrome, which motivated medieval church theologians to distrust, fear, and even hate women. If women aren't seducing righteous men of God now, they are at the least destroying their sexuality and weakening their wills.

Christianity Today magazine recently carried an article on why men leave the ministry. One of the reasons cited was that they had been duped, seduced, and destroyed by scheming women. The author overlooked the fact that these men could have said no. This is the same specious argument that those crooked congressmen used in the Abscam scandal. "I was tricked, seduced. I'm not to blame. If the temptation hadn't been there, I wouldn't have fallen." Naturally. Who couldn't say that about any sin he had committed? The excuse is as old as Adam, and just as morally corrupt now as it was then. It's also a sudden, and too convenient, plea of powerlessness.

But the root of all this is a loss of power. So, if the man is losing his power in the home, he may be more determined than ever not to lose it where he works. We could rephrase "barefoot, hungry, and pregnant" to read "keep them poorly paid, eager, and overworked." There are many tactics to keep a woman in her place in the work force. Most of them can be summed up in two words: sexual harassment. It may be illegal, it may be immoral, but it exists—in Christian organizations as well as in secular. Although it has very little to do with sex, it has a great deal to do with power.

Most women, who have been raised to expect men to behave in a certain way, often don't realize that they are being sexually harassed. They also haven't been trained in confrontation or psychological contact, which is "unladylike, unfeminine behavior."

When I was nineteen I worked in a mostly male office. One of the men was a Christian, and I sometimes attended his church. The other men were not. With the exception of the Christian, these men constantly made sexual jokes at my expense, commented on my physical appearance, and asked pointed, rude sexual questions. It embarrassed me. It made me uncomfortable. These are not uncommon reactions of a woman who is being sexually harassed. Because I did not know what to say, I said nothing. I thought that if I ignored the remarks, the men would stop. They didn't, and there was nothing I could do about it.

During the months I had this job, my fellow Christian said nothing on my behalf, so one day I said something to him at lunch. I told him I didn't like what was going on. He told me that it was *my* fault, that because I had never said anything to the men everyone assumed that I liked it. He thought that I had encouraged their harassment. I couldn't believe what I was hearing. He, of course, said that he disapproved of their behavior, but it wasn't his place to say anything, especially since I was to blame. They were, after all, men.

This Christian man was participating as much as if he had verbally assaulted me, too. But I did take his advice. The next time one of the men started his harassment, I told him I didn't like it, that I was offended, and asked him to stop it. That only made him more interested. I suppose I had aroused his instinct for challenge and conquest.

Several things were happening in this situation. As a lowly typist I had no power. As a female, and an object, my powerlessness was reinforced. This harassment made it difficult for me to do my job, and I believe my work, if not bad, was at least mediocre. In the afternoons, I supervised a group of high school business students. I was supposed to see that they typed a certain number of pages a day. You might call that a position of some authority, but it was undermined because of the attitude of those men who supervised me. Although the incident occurred fifteen years ago, it still happens to women every day all across the country.

A kissing cousin to sexual harassment is the refusal to find, develop, and promote talented women. The reasons often given in Christian organizations differ little from those of secular business. (There are some notable exceptions.)

Sometimes a woman who deserves a promotion is not given it because her male colleagues would be jealous, hurt, threatened, or embittered. It doesn't matter when promoting a male that other males may feel jealous, hurt, threatened, or embittered. That's something they must live with. But few men will risk provoking those feelings in another man by promoting a woman. A woman also may find it difficult to do her job because someone fears the appearance of evil. Certainly we should avoid anything that could be misinterpreted, but at a certain point a company must say that evil is in the eye of the beholder. These so-called problems are excuses as to why companies can't hire women. It could be summed up by saying that women can't operate as equals and therefore are ineffective.

Faced with such barriers, women often resort to using sexuality to gain power. How? Let's look again at a simple male/female relationship. Although a man takes the initiative, a clever woman may manipulate him into doing what she wants by using her sexuality. Even avoiding premarital intercourse may be done simply to heighten a man's desires and to assure a marriage proposal. The letter of the law, yes, but hardly the spirit. Many Christian mothers have impressed on their daughters that sex is their only, or greatest, weapon in the power struggle between the sexes. Although all books on sex and marriage urge that sex not be used as a weapon, a woman may find it difficult to relinquish, if she believes and has been raised to believe that it is the only way to gain and maintain power. Of course, men, too, can use sex within marriage for power, but it takes the opposite form. Rather than withholding sex, he insists on it as his right or due, thus showing his wife "who is boss," another way of saying "I have the power." More and more, marriage and family counselors are recognizing that the fight for power is a basic underlying problem in marriage, which can and does, take many forms.

The subtle variations of using sexuality for power can be effective in many contexts, including a business one. A woman can evoke a sexual response by the colors she wears, the texture of the fabrics she chooses, the scent of her perfume, the cut and shape of a dress, skirt, blouse. Men have a uniform—a three-piece suit. Women don't. Even a business suit on a woman can aid in a sexual ploy for power.

A woman can gain much with this. First, and most important, she can become noticed: She wants to get the right kind of attention, of course, the kind that will provide her a platform to display her work. In certain circumstances, she might try to disconcert a colleague or superior so that his mind wanders and she can step in with suggestions or solutions to a problem. A woman might decide to threaten a male colleague psychologically with her sexual presence, thus keeping him fearful and off-balance around her. This is not overtly, obviously immoral behavior. There is no question here of promiscuity—just some subtle body language, perhaps, or an expression, a clever use of a voice or eyes or figure.

Nearly anyone can use their sexuality to gain power. They needn't be beautiful or handsome, just clever. Then there are the relatives of sexuality, the little girl/little boy ploys that work so well. A capable woman can make a little continued helplessness take her far. Women *and* men will rush to her aid. Suddenly, she's in control, people are doing what she wants, and only later may someone wonder how it all happened. A judicious use of tears can serve the same purpose, though that may only work once; but once may be enough. Those who see her tears may be so cowed that the mere threat of tears later may serve just as well. A hurt, vulnerable expression on a grown man can and has moved

many a woman. An anguished cry for help, especially if the cry is
phrased in such a way that the victim feels that he or she alone is
the person to help, can also be effective.

No one can be quite comfortable thinking of these means to
power; it cuts us too close to the bone, because almost every one
of us has been guilty of using our sexuality in some way to
manipulate and control others. Sexual response between men and
women is always present and nearly automatic. We need to
recognize this, and though we can't dispel it completely, we can
avoid deliberately using sexuality for power. Although that
sounds easy, it isn't, even when we are conscious of the ploys we
use.

There is nothing more discouraging than to leave a situation
knowing you have resorted to certain sexual tricks. A young
female executive never understood how she could use a silly, yet
seductive, giggle and a soft roll of her eyes to sway an uncon-
vinced male colleague "to see things her way." But there it
was—her training from an early age learned at her mother's knee
and perfected at her father's. "I'm just a silly female," she
seemed to say. "Humor me." Yet she was anything but—she
was professional, tough, knowledgeable, and imaginative. It was
easier, though, to win through sexual manipulation than face her
male colleagues as equals. She knew that to do that, though it
would have been honest, would probably have meant failure. She
was not paid to fail. You're not; I'm not. We have put so high a
premium on success that we unthinkingly choose the most expedient insurance against failure. We are judged by our pro-
ductivity, not always by our honesty. And the quickest way to
success or achievement in a male/female working relationship is
the sexual ploy.

This is so insidious that perhaps only we, or we and our object,
understand what's happening. Maybe our instinctive use of our
sexuality is beyond our conscious recognition of it. Women may

believe that's really all they have. They've been taught this in
school, in church, and in the home. Both aspects of our culture
—the secular and the sacred—have reinforced that a woman is
powerless except in one area.

Consider the numerous books in the last decade that have im-
plicitly promoted sex for power as the *biblical* mandate for
women. Marabel Morgan wasn't the first, nor will she be the last,
to encourage women to sexually play on their husbands for—to
use some of Morgan's examples—new refrigerators, fancy vaca-
tions, or furniture. The husband is lulled into sexual senseless-
ness. Who has the power? The woman. She knows what she
wants and she knows how to get it.

The trick is a good one, because while she is getting what she
wants, the man thinks, "Well, I don't know what happened, but
she finally understands who's in charge here." For this sexual
ploy to work the woman must seem to give the man what he
wants—no arguments, no disagreeable sights, sounds, or smells,
no bruised male ego. But the woman has reduced the man to an
object, a toy; he has become nonhuman. The woman is indeed
total—totally powerful over her husband's life as it relates to her.
In this, she becomes like God, which is ultimately what we want
from power, to become the God of our universe.

On the other side, we have those like Bill Gothard, who help
men use their sexuality as a means to power: strength, will,
intellectual or spiritual force, all those attributes that we traditionally have thought of as "masculine." The adjunct to this is
that women love (substitute "are excited by," "submit to") men
who take charge. Here, the woman becomes nonhuman.

Whether women are becoming more wary, or men more obvious, the machismo tactics seem less successful. But that doesn't
mean that a man's sexual means to power is disappearing. It is
being revamped and redirected. A man doesn't shout a woman
into subservience; he cajoles her. He soothes her with gifts and
soft words. Insinuate yourself, a man is told—you can catch
more flies with honey than vinegar. The rewards will be beyond
your wildest imaginings. You'll have a sexual tiger who also
knows her place. You won't have to fight for the kingdom; she'll
willingly put you on the throne.

Because life doesn't separate easily into compartments, how we behave in one area of our life will affect how we act in another. Home life and office life and church life flow together. With some modifications of propriety, good taste, and morality, what is the pattern in one place will be the pattern in another. Failure to recognize this is a basic problem with all the books that promote sexual manipulation to gain power over a mate. Yes, they work; if they work in one context they might easily work in another. What's a small pat on the shoulder or squeeze on the arm in the office? Innocent or offputting? Does it keep the other person slightly ill-at-ease and unable to concentrate? Well, it's not our fault if a little hug lowers the person's performance. The person probably has a spiritual problem if he (she) can't keep his (her) mind pure, goes the reasoning.

The point of such behavior is to keep the other person off-balance. In Christian organizations it is almost never intended to be a subtle way to arouse another's interest. In fact, sexual tactics are far more effective when used to irritate or deprecate someone. It is a way of saying, "You are not worth anything but as an object of my power." When this is done by a man to a woman in an office, he is saying to her that she is beneath him treating her as fully human. She is _only_ a woman.

When a woman does this to a man, she is saying that he is a simpleton, who can be easily duped. Once a woman knows how to play to the proverbially tender male ego, her position of power is secure. And what woman hasn't had good and early training in this? Or, if a woman wants to move ahead but thinks she may threaten the male who will say yes or no to her promotion, it is easy enough to reassure him that while she loves her work and would like to serve the company to her fullest ability, her real joy is in those little domestic tasks that most men love women to do. She just crosses her legs, leans forward a little, alters her tone of voice, and admits how she loves to cook. Somehow cooking and female sexuality seem, in our culture, to be synonyms—perhaps because they are both physical. The man is disarmed; her power is secure. She has put herself in a nonthreatening role.

Such behavior is demeaning. We demean ourselves when we practice sexual exploitation for power. We demean the person we are practicing *on*. We are treating a fellow creature in a way that disregards his immortality. We have tried to dampen the glory that rightly belongs to another. God sees that person as a little lower than the angels. He sees us, amazing as it sounds, in the same way. When we fail to treat another that way, we violate God's law.

Humanity is holy; our neighbors and co-workers are part of that holiness. Christ became humanity. He said to us, "When you have done it unto the least of these my brethren, you have done it unto me." We need to consider for our soul's sake what it is we do to "the least of these."

6.

6.
POWER THROUGH PIETY

*Most, if not all, of the mischief in the world is
done in the name of righteousness.*
—Robert Farrar Capon, *The Third Peacock*

To Christians alone comes the temptation to use piety for power,
for in our ecclesiastical culture the more spiritual a person is, the
more powerful he is. Spirituality brings followers. And the more
followers one has, obviously the more spiritual one must be. The
cycle repeats itself, making one even more powerful with more
followers. The cassock of righteousness becomes the vestment of
power. There is something in us that wants to associate with the
powerful or admit someone into the ranks of the powerful because of dress, manner, appearance, affluence, or contacts. Most
of us simultaneously hold two strikingly different attitudes. Part
of us longs for the freedom and influence we think power can
give; and part of us longs to relinquish our freedom and influence
to someone who will give us answers to our problems. One
Savior, no matter how much we proclaim to the contrary, is not
enough. We need others whom we can see and touch. But in
giving a person such power, we give him no gift, but a burden.
We have made that person into what he had no right to be and
cannot support, no matter how hard he tries; we have made him
into a god.

But what of those people who want power and who use spiritual manipulation, intrigue, guilt, prayer, badgering, righteousness, and sanctimonious language to get it? Let's take a familiar scene. You are in a church meeting. Perhaps the church is trying to decide whether or not to start a building program, or buy an organ, or call a new pastor. The issue could be more controversial—whether or not to ordain a woman minister or deacon or whether to accept as members a racially mixed couple (yes, some churches still have to ask that question). You and your fellow congregants may be undecided. But what happens when one or two vocal, intense people express a preference? First, their opinions are always phrased in spiritual language: "After much prayer . . . ," "Having searched the Scriptures . . . ," "The Lord has told me . . . ," and so forth. Second, in such a situation those are the people whose opinions usually prevail at the meeting, often over the better judgment of others, and over people who truly are spiritual. True spirituality is a habit of being that doesn't draw attention to itself.

Exactly why is a person or group of people considered "spiritual" and thus able to gain power? Church attendance might head the list—as often as the church is open. Visibility, which insures that they will be known, is important. An astute observer can quickly decide who wields the power in a local church. Near the top of the list could also be how much the person or group contributes to the church budget. Do they tithe? Or give more than 10 percent? Is this giving generally known? Then, there are other factors like prayer, Bible study, and pietistic language.

All of these can be sincere manifestations of someone trying to live the Christlike life. But they can also be the means by which someone gains power. They also may have nothing to do with true spirituality. Christ castigated the Pharisees for their ostentatious religious dress, public prayers, visible piety, and outward purity. They tithed with flair, but were filled with dead men's bones. Their language was always sanctimonious, but their words were the trumpets of hypocrisy. Christ also talked about the desirability of doing good works in secret and being rewarded in secret.

Unfortunately, those to whom we give power in the church are more likely to be those who look, sound, and act spiritual. These highly visible people seem in sharp contrast to the models Christ offered us—models of powerlessness: the widow who humbly gave all she had, the poor sinner who prayed secretly and in earnest. Jesus commanded us to strive for anonymity, not visibility. Those who want power and strive for it by parading piety violate his command. As with the Pharisees who wore their spiritual clothes with relish—for the garments proclaimed authority to those around them—we often do the same. But our clothes of authority by which we claim power may be no more than who we know or what position we hold.

Authority is a marvelous, dangerous word, behind which many a power-hungry person hides, believing that authority gives him the right to rule others, to have others acquiesce to his views of spiritual right and wrong. When I was growing up, I heard many sermons about "authority in the pulpit." I discovered that what the minister really meant was that he intended to use his power to get his way. Generally he got it, often to the church's dismay. Although Protestant churches have since the Reformation decried the power of the Pope, we have always had many little popes.

The difficulty lies with the meaning of the words _power_ and _authority_. We think of them as synonymous; they are not. Power means insistence on what we want for no other reason than that we want it; it means making other people follow us despite their own wishes. Power is assumed, insensitive, dehumanizing, and ultimately destructive. Authority, on the other hand, is positive, and usually involves a conferred right within strictly controlled bounds. It is a temporary recognition or a temporary state of "in-chargeness." A traffic cop has authority when the lights aren't working, but no real power in and of himself, which he and we would soon discover if he acted outside his authority to signal which cars should turn left, which should wait, and which should go straight ahead. We can also see the difference between power and authority in the relationship between parent and child. A

parent can exercise power over his child—"you do what I tell
you because I'm in charge"—or authority, where he leads his
child into understanding and maturity. There is a visible difference in relationships, depending on which approach is used.
Authority is not a personal attribute, but something that is
always separate from the person and that can be given to another.
Only in the Trinity are power and authority combined. Even
there, though, we might say that Christ's authority is conferred
on him by the Father. Even though Christ exercised authority
over the wind and the seas, over creation itself, he said that he
could perform no miracles, heal no bodies—thus changing and
entering another human being—without the person's permission.
He refused to operate with unilateral power. The Grand Inquisitor
in *The Brothers Karamazov* indicted Christ just because he had
not done so. Jesus knew, though, that he was not to compete for
power on the same level as the Romans. To do so would have
meant accepting the Romans' definition of power—one of coercion and violence. Christ could not do so without negating his
purpose; righteousness and power cannot march together.

This linguistic tangle between authority and power is a difficult
one to untwist. The two are so close, and have been synonymous
in our culture for so long, that they are now hard to separate. The
exercise of power always implies coercion and violence because
the purpose of power is to reproduce itself. Whatever tries to
prevent this reproduction must be disposed of. An exercise of
authority, however, should have nothing to do with coercion,
violence, or manipulation. Yet in our zeal for God's work we
decide that if someone won't recognize our authority, we will
force him to with our power. Although Paul talked about using
any means to win people to Christ, he didn't mean violence,
manipulation, or coercion, which is intended to change another
person. Paul wanted the message-bearer to adapt *himself* to his
audience. For example, when preaching to uneducated people,
don't show all your intellectual acumen. It is a matter of focus.
There are many kinds of violence. We are often guilty of violence
against the spirit or the intellect. Whereas God allows us frail
creatures to question him and meander as best we can from darkness into light—the Psalms are filled with examples of people

struggling to believe God—we simply can't allow that.

People who use spiritual violence are hiding behind authority to gain power. This all-too-common practice works partly because we have confused the meaning of the two words. If someone claims authority—here we are not talking about authority conferred but authority taken or usurped—we assume that he has the power to run over us with his view of spiritual reality.

In this context, the tools of power are someone's spiritual benchmarks. He may talk about his devotional life, the hours he spends in prayer, or his rising early for his hour or two of Bible study. He may drop the names of important spiritual people he knows and socializes with. He tithes with a flourish. He attends meetings assiduously. He witnesses vigorously. He always speaks authoritatively—as if his opinions arrived fresh from heaven each day. None of these things are evil, which is why they are so hard to discern. Yet they become evil when used to say "I am more spiritual; listen to me. I know the mind of the Lord." There was a reason for Christ's command to do our good deeds in secret. He understood our natures.

During the height of the charismatic movement in the seventies, I attended the "First International Conference on the Holy Spirit" in Jerusalem as a reporter. Most of the attendees spoke in tongues and were convinced that someone wasn't "completely" a Christian if he didn't. Since I was not a charismatic, I became the object of much witnessing. People badgered me about speaking in tongues (there is no other way to describe it). One otherwise charming elderly woman told me that God had sent me to the conference just so I would begin to speak in tongues. And there were others, not quite as charming, who upbraided me for not submitting to the Holy Spirit, for being proud and defensive. These people wanted power over my relationship to God. They used every spiritual tactic they could think of to shame, harass, embarrass, and propel me into an experience that was for them the mark of a Christian. These people were guilty of spiritual violence and thus of misplaced loyalty: The wrong god was in control.

That experience made me aware of how non-Christians must feel when Christians use much the same techniques to convince them they should convert. We use fear, anger, persuasion, hostility, debate, tears. We try in effect to run their lives. We forget that God is the only one who has a right to power. We forget our place by trying to usurp his.

A great part of this spiritual manipulation comes from the language we use. The word comes to us easily—as by birth or right. "God gave me the power." "I speak in the power of the Spirit." We read certain Bible verses, such as 2 Corinthians 4:7, but I'm not sure we know what they really mean, or can admit that they show how powerless we are in relation to the All-Powerful. How many of us really think of ourselves as "jars of clay," as Paul calls us, weak vessels, earthenware? Don't we see instead, Royal Doulton China and Reed & Barton sterling silver?

Although we use the word *power* in a spiritual context, we invest it with a secular meaning, which then subtly changes the way we think of certain spiritual concepts. If power means manipulation, or a quality that will bring us what we want, then the idea of prayer, for example, is transformed from worship and faith to a mere talisman, a tool for gaining our desires. We speak of the Bible in much the same way.

When we talk about "God's power in us," what we really mean is that we have become powerful and allowed God to share in a little of the glory. We have made the right moves, developed the right contacts, and quoted the right Scriptures. We have spiritually intimidated those under or around us. We have declared ourselves right and others wrong. To reinforce our image, we talk about how God has prospered us. No one likes to argue with someone once God is mentioned. We also thus prevent scrutiny of how we treat our friends, neighbors, spouses, or colleagues. We intercept the uncomfortable questions.

But if uncomfortable questions should come despite our best precautions, we already have a defense, another form of spiritual violence. We can hint that the person asking the questions is spiritually immature or suffering from a divisive spirit, a troublemaker. We indicate that he needs "to get right with God." He doesn't have the interests of the church (or the company) at heart.

He is out to gain power himself. And if those insinuations don't silence him, we can always say, "I think we'd better pray about your problem." There is no end to the spiritual harassment that a power-hungry person can accomplish. The one at the receiving end has no resource at his disposal. Any answer will merely make him seem more and more defensive, and thus more and more wrong.

Please don't misunderstand. I am not saying that to prove you _aren't_ power-grasping you should avoid prayer, never quote Scripture, skip church, and so forth. It isn't the presence of all these that indicates a love of power; it is the consistent, regular use and abuse of them to further a person's desires—despite the consequences to the spirit of another. This can happen in a church, in a business, or in a home. It is arrogance at its worst. We have all been guilty of it.

Some of us still are.

7.

7.
POWER FACE TO FACE

Power is the most serious problem in Christianity today.

—Ted Engstrom

The busy floor of the Christian Bookseller's Convention is a strange and noisy place to conduct an interview. Yet, it provided a good backdrop for the subject, *What is power?* As did the office of the chairman of the board of a large sign corporation in Nashville, Tennessee. Or the press room of one of the congressional buildings on Capitol Hill. Or the spacious office of a vice-president at General Motors.

In preparing the material for this book, I have talked with many, many Christians—businessmen and women, ministers, teachers, theologians, writers, housewives. These discussions often took the form of formal interviews, but some were held over coffee or from the back seat of a car. Whoever the people were, and wherever and however we talked, one thing was quite clear: everyone is fascinated by the subject of power. Everyone has a strong opinion as to what it is, how it operates, and what should be the proper Christian attitude toward it.

Some people had never considered the subject before I raised it. Others had spent their lives in the middle of it. A few were concerned that they didn't seem to want power—that they didn't actively seek it or promote themselves in order to get it. Perhaps, they wondered, they weren't doing all that God intended them to. Then there were those for whom there was no question as to whether power was the proper sphere for Christians; the question just had never come up. Some people wondered why *I* wondered about power. What was I afraid of? At least one person accused me of naïveté and oversimplification—or of overstating the problem. I'm not yet ready to plead guilty.

Although the people I talked with represent a variety of professions and interests, nearly everyone agreed about the definition of power: the ability to influence others, to convince others to think or do what you would like them to think or do (the *you* being the person with the power). The surprise to me was that most of them believed that using power was essential, not just for business people or ministers, but for everyone. They saw the real issue as being the morality of behavior—how well we use power and for what reason.

This was stated most clearly by the two business people I interviewed, Dr. Betsy Ancker-Johnson, a vice-president of General Motors, and Fred Smith, an independent businessman from Texas who now writes a column for *Leadership* magazine. Ancker-Johnson is in a unique position, being a Christian, a woman, and an executive in a now-struggling industry.

When I asked Ancker-Johnson about power—what she thought it was, whether it was legitimate to use, and whether she did use it—she admitted that she had never really thought about it. For one thing, she had never intended to go into management, but had planned to stay in research. It was when she decided that pure research had lost its sharpest challenge for her that she thought about a management job. For an executive, though, power becomes an issue. Executives must ensure that all the jobs under their care are done, which is how Ancker-Johnson sees herself functioning. She has to convince her employees that what she wants done is their idea—that being the best way to accomplish the task. She always hopes that such persuasion will work. She admits to manipulating her employees, if necessary. This is also part of her job as an executive, she believes. Ancker-Johnson is paid to use power. Although she hopes that an outright order will not be necessary, the subtler tactics of persuasion, manipulation, and maneuvering being more comfortable, it sometimes is.

She believes that the theological principles of stewardship demand that she conduct her professional life as she does. She is paid to do a job, she says, and she must do it with whatever means are at her disposal. She also strongly believes that God ordered us to power when he commanded Adam and Eve to be fruitful and multiply, to fill the earth and subdue it. For Ancker-Johnson the important word is "subdue," a word that calls us to power, because without power, we can't get anything done.

Fred Smith essentially agrees with Ancker-Johnson about the function of power for a Christian executive. Smith who had thought a great deal about power, adds something to the definitions of power: "It's the ability to either cause something to happen or to keep something from happening. . . . It's also the opportunity to act without restraint. The absence of restraint is nearer the evidence of power than any other thing I've thought about." People want power, says Smith, because they want responsibility; the two go together.

"Power is so multi-faceted. There is the power of charisma, the power of lethargy, the power of silence, the power of election—I have never been able to say 'this is power,' unless you want to go all the way back to God. Probably the original energy is the original power, but it's been perverted." Yet, Smith doesn't believe that power is a quality that someone owns innately and that propels him into the circumstance of power. For him, we cannot know power apart from circumstances. One day one kind of person is powerful, the next day someone else. He also sees power in the abstract—that is power in potential, not being acted out.

We discussed the relationship between power and authority. "Authority," says Smith, "is a conferred, assumed power. Authority is conferred on somebody. We assume that authority carries the power inherent in the authority. Very often it doesn't carry that power." But the fault lies not with the authority, which comes from power, but with a person's fear of using power.

Which is why Smith would never promote someone who didn't want power. "I don't see how you can accomplish anything without power—now, I'm talking about organizational power, of course." To him, promoting someone who rejects the notion of power would be like someone "buying a new car who was afraid to buy gasoline. It would be a beautiful thing, but it wouldn't run." And what of the drive to get power in order to see things run? "I don't think that you have to go through machinations or nonsense to get power. I don't have that view at all. It seems to me that power is just part of the necessary equipment for doing a good job."

So Christians who want to do something must strive for power? I asked. Here he hesitated. "I don't know how you're going to do anything—well, I don't think you have to strive for power. I think power comes as you try to do things. I don't see this drive for power that you seem to fear. Power to me is just as natural as gasoline in the automobile. And I treat it just as normally. I agree that some people become drunk on power. . . . but I think that the desire for power is necessary, not to aggrandize myself, but in order to accomplish. I think this is legitimate for a Christian."

And dangerous? Yes, says Smith, "power is dangerous. It's like electricity. You must keep it insulated." You also must ensure, somehow, that you are using power properly, since it is so dangerous. In this, honesty is crucial. "Being human I doubt that I can be honest. But I can keep from consciously being dishonest. And that's about as high as I can go."

Conversations about power that lasted several hours are hard to distill in a limited space, and yet these few comments touch on the basic issues. What is power? Why do we want it? What is the relationship between power and authority? What is the Christian position? Ancker-Johnson and Smith perceive power from a typically American, or perhaps Western, position: pragmatism. Throughout both interviews, the prospect of not getting things done was the greatest fear expressed. If using power in some way helps people get things done, then that becomes a mandate for Christians. Otherwise, we violate another principle: not doing that for which we receive compensation—which, in Smith's view, is legal embezzlement.

Shortly after I talked with Fred Smith, he sent me some un-
published material from a friend of his, a minister. His friend was
studying the story of Joseph and his brothers, looking for light on
the meaning of power. The sermon attempts to prove that power
is "not evil, but a stewardship." As with money, power can be
used for good or ill. The interesting thing about his argument was
that with every point the minister added warnings about places
where power can get out of control and times when people use
power incorrectly. Underneath his theory that we can and are
commanded to use power is the implied reality that we are simply
incapable of doing so, even when our motivations are right.

Robert Farrar Capon in _The Third Peacock_ makes this cogent
observation: "The human race adheres devoutly to the belief
that one more application of power will bring in the kingdom. . . . For a long time—since the Fall, in fact—man has
been in love with the demonic style of power. For a somewhat
shorter time, he has enjoyed, or suffered from, the possession of
vast resources of power. Where has it gotten him?"
Power is everywhere for the taking. Why shouldn't Christians
have as much, if not more, than the non-Christians? As Christians, won't we use power better? Yet we don't seem that much
better off for having power.
Historian George Marsden has traced the changes that have
occurred in fundamentalism during this century. He notes that
there is a striking difference in the desire of fundamentalism today
for power. Or, as Robert Webber of Wheaton College might put it,
fundamentalists and some evangelicals are buying into a political
power structure, which is essentially anti-Christian, believing that
by so doing they can transform the structure.
It is a short step from using power in a secular, perhaps political, setting to employing the same methods in Christian organizations, in the church, or in the family. If the methods work one
place, they'll surely work in another. If we can, politically, turn
stones into bread and thus capture people, can't we use the same
approach to turn water into wine to win allegiance?

Ted Engstrom, now president of World Vision and on the boards of several major Christian organizations, thinks that power ought to have a negative connotation for Christians. The difficulty, says Engstrom, is that it is also a biblical word. Because Scripture uses the word to define the acts, or the energy, of the Trinity, we fail to realize that too often we are using it secularly, rather than Christianly. Engstrom firmly believes that it has been misused in evangelical circles. Too many of us, he says, equate power with influence, money, and position. "And that is a faulty thing; we are doing what the world is doing—'stones into bread to bind people to us.'" In defining power, Engstrom emphasizes a person's use of his *own* money, influence, or position—whether for good or evil. The problem lies with it being seen as something we possess. We know, at least intellectually, that we cannot possess God's power. We receive it by his grace. Engstrom is deeply concerned about the increasing use of secular power in the church and sees the problem most acutely with those media celebrities whom Quebedeaux so incisively analyzes in *By What Authority?* According to Engstrom, these people "have begun to believe their own press releases."

Engstrom agrees that people who use power mistakenly believe that only with and through power can they "get ahead." He struggles with the difficulty of being part of a so-called powerful organization. It puts a burden on the people who make up the organization to maintain the servant role—which is, after all, the reason for the existence of such organizations as World Vision. "I would rather be less visible and smaller in order to do more effective work in the church," he says. He thinks that their size, influence, and financial wherewithal at times interferes with their work. People can fear an organization because of those things. "Organizations as well as individuals," adds Engstrom, "must evaluate whether it will play a servant role, which is a very difficult thing to do, or whether it will continue down the power path."

Engstrom's view of power is quite different from most of the other people I spoke with. He believes that it is possible to be a good manager or executive without a hunger for power. But Engstrom also doesn't equate the roles of leadership and management. A leader, he says, is in greater danger of succumbing to power than a manager. Managing, he believes, is the job of delegating work and encouraging and developing people. That might take good interpersonal skills, but it does not take power. Good interpersonal skills and manipulation are not synonyms, however. Too often people assume they are. Manipulation is a tool of power; encouraging people to do their best is not. As a management expert, Engstrom thinks that resorting to manipulation is a dangerous practice. A manipulative manager is self-serving, not other-serving. Personal example, not the use of power, makes good executives. Leaders, on the other hand, may exude a certain aura, or charisma, that people mistake for power; the people then accord these leaders the treatment due power.

In rejecting the notion that a good executive must have a desire for power to succeed, Engstrom believes that "the Christian executive, the Christian manager, needs to be one who is willing to subjugate himself, to bury himself in other people. And that means you must be willing to nullify yourself over and over again." The misconception comes in the way we view our jobs. We are not to make ourselves look good, but to make our superior, our staff, and our associates look good. Although Christians should be especially conscious of this, Engstrom doesn't see this practiced very often, either by Christians in secular business or those working in Christian organizations.

Engstrom, who is peculiarly suited to observe the trends in Christian management after almost forty-five years of experience, believes that this hunger for power is increasing. "It's the worst it's been at any time during my career," he says. Yet it is possible to be a powerful person and be unconscious of that power. Charles E. Fuller was such a person. At the Berlin Congress in 1966, says Engstrom, after Fuller was introduced, people stood and applauded him. "It utterly amazed him. He couldn't understand why they were doing that," says Engstrom. That, he adds, is the kind of powerful person we don't see very often today.

Unfortunately, Engstrom concludes, this problem of power is inescapable—especially today, when people are longing for hero-leaders. "It is almost forced upon leaders. The pastor of a large church is in danger when he is put on a pedestal. The voice of the person on radio or television suffers from it." Engstrom draws a lesson from Scripture. He asks us to look at the people Jesus chose to be his disciples. The only well-known man was Matthew, and he wasn't well-liked. Advice? Engstrom urges us to seek role models in Scripture or in people like Fuller or A. W. Tozer. And he tells us to be willing to evaluate ourselves, to look at our behavior hard, if we want to be servant leaders—which is really the only choice for a Christian.

Both Charles Colson and Wesley Pippert have been part of the most visible avenue of power—government.

Pippert, as longtime correspondent for United Press International, sees power as "a reality in the world and we must deal with it." Everyone, he says, from the top leaders in government to the traffic cop at 13th and G streets in Washington, exercises power. "Power comes from God and is morally neutral. . . . The world often uses power to manipulate, to impose, to force in sinful ways. . . . But the Bible almost always uses its concept of power in a loving, caring, enhancing way. . . . God's use of power is a model for us."

Pippert says the enforcement of laws and a well-ordered society demand that certain people have power. (In this context, I would say these people need authority, not power.) How would society function otherwise? he wonders. Which brings us back again to the issue of getting things done.

Sometimes it might be better to leave things undone than to achieve them by the means of power. Colson finally realized this after his conversion. In *Born Again,* he recounts many incidents where he got things done in his job at the White House. He learned quickly how to cut through red tape to accomplish difficult tasks. He wasn't really doing it for his own power—or at least he thought he wasn't. His motivation was of the highest. "I was very idealistic in my beliefs about what government should accomplish," he explains. Power being the "ability to influence others" means that whatever influences people—money, political office, personality—equals power.

Colson sees the church and the political arena as much more

similar than we would like to think. "The church can be a vehicle of power. If someone is honest with himself, he's got to admit it to be one of the terrific struggles of the Christian church. We breed a form of egomania not unlike politicians. There are a lot of comparables; for example, the ability to influence others when you're preaching a sermon or when you're exhorting people to do things as a pastor."

A politician, says Colson, thrives on the adulation of a crowd. And a minister or Christian leader can respond in the same way. Until he became active in Christian ministry, Colson was never the man out front, but always the man behind the scenes. Now, he is in demand as a public Christian figure. He confesses that he likes it, even though he wouldn't have chosen it for himself. "I have mixed feelings. I worry about the fact that I like the attention. I don't know what keeps the Christian leader humble. You can become an egomaniac in this business. That's why I often preach and write about Christ's words that if you seek your life you'll lose it, but if you seek to lose your life, you'll find it."

So what keeps Colson in balance? His willingness to give up the public attention and notoriety his prison ministry is giving him in secular, as well as Christian, circles. "If I become dependent on this, then I must leave it. I've had a lot of power, and I saw how empty it was. I don't think I could get sucked into that again. On the other hand, I realize how much I needed it once in my life, so I will never be sure that I won't need it again."

Colson's comments are perhaps the most pointed; of all the people I spoke with, he had had the most power. It corrupted him despite himself. He thought, as many of us think, that as long as our motivation is worthy, we can use power without fear. But, as Colson and others of us could testify, power just doesn't work that way.

8.

8.
SO WHAT DOES
THE BIBLE SAY?

Now power is of its nature evil, whoever wields it. It is not stability but a lust, and ipso facto *insatiable, therefore unhappy in itself and doomed to make others unhappy.*

—Jakob Burchhardt

Martin Hengel in his little book *Christ and Power* makes a telling observation about certain influences on our culture. Sociologists and psychologists, he says, have insisted that a desire for power, "the striving to have one's own desire for authority, to acquire one's own space to move about freely [thus constricting the freedom of others], *is basic to every healthy person, not least the so-called intellectual"* (italics added). This is the culture in which Christians live, and it has affected our theology.

In striving to change the world, or at least influence it for good, we have accommodated our theology to the world. Sacrifice, commitment, service, and discipline—qualities that invigorate and strengthen those who practice them—have been replaced, or downplayed, by a Christian "do your own thing," or to use the spiritual phrase, "fulfilling your gifts."

Christ *has* promised abundant life, and he has given each of us certain abilities to use for furthering his kingdom. We do have the parable of the talents and of the hard steward to instruct us. But the motivation in this new wave of pop psychology/theology is slightly off-center. The biblical purpose for fulfilling our gifts is to benefit God's work; that we are fulfilled in doing so is a by-product, not its raison d'être. Unfortunately it is the experience itself that has become valid and valuable, rather than the furtherance of the kingdom. Whether or not we like what God has given us to do is not relevant; we should still do it. There are always aspects of any project that we find tiring or irritating. Without commitment to the person for whom we work, a firm belief that he has called us to it, and a discipline to get the job done regardless of our feelings, we would accomplish little.

This is an unpopular view of Christianity. Surely Christ wants us to do what we want and be happy while we are doing it. Isn't he there to help us and back us up? We don't go to Christ to submit ourselves to his discipline. He comes to us bearing gifts. This is the reverse of biblical theology. We hear that Christ belongs to us, not we to him. We are told that he fulfills our desires; we do not fulfill his.

When Norman Vincent Peale originally preached the power of positive thinking, evangelicals were certain that he did not preach the whole gospel. Now Robert Schuller preaches the power of possibility thinking—a semantic difference only from what Peale preached—and thousands flock to the Crystal Cathedral on Sundays and millions more watch him on television. These men preach a gospel—of power; they are not alone. And they claim that the manual of power is the Bible.

Is it? Or does the Bible speak of power in a different way and in another context?

Scripture includes many instances of the use and misuse of power. The Old Testament gives instructive examples of how God looks at power. Jesus talked a great deal about power; and the disciples were certainly concerned about it. Paul encountered its effects and in certain of his missionary journeys was involved in power struggles, not necessarily of his own making.

Along with the events of Scripture, we should look at the historical context in which they occurred. We can discover much about the Bible's view of power by considering the political situation in which the patriarchs and prophets lived; what the first century was like when Jesus preached in Galilee and Judea; and how the political and religious balance shifted during the development of the early church.

From the first day of creation, men and women have faced the problem of power. It was the desire to be powerful—to be like God—that caused Adam and Eve to disobey the Lord. Satan understood from firsthand experience how great was the call of power: He fell from heaven because he longed to be greater than he was. Ever since he has used power to tempt men and women as he tempted Adam and Eve. The disguises may be good, but they all hide one desire. Even the murder of Abel stemmed from it. Cain could not bear to have his brother above him. Cain's lack of power led him to fratricide.

Even the flood waters of God did not destroy man's desire for power. On the plain in Shinar men again tried to transcend their divinely appointed limitations. They wanted to be free to name themselves, free from outside power, and thus free to assume their own power. The Tower of Babel was the monument of their desire.*

Although the patriarchs lived before Israel became a nation, they faced many political difficulties. God had called Abraham to leave the civilized, cultured city Ur to travel a rough, unknown land. He had been told that this land would belong to him and his descendants—which presented a problem of power for Abraham. He knew what God had said; the inhabitants of Canaan did not.

Foreigners had no rights—not even water or burial rights. The former was a life-sustaining necessity, the latter a cultural one. Abraham solved the problem of water rights by making a treaty with Abimelech (see Gen. 21:22–32). But until he owned land, Abraham was still a stranger. After he bought the cave of Machpelah near Mamre—where he buried Sarah, and where he, Isaac, and Jacob were buried—he had a power base to legitimize his claim to Canaan. God was fulfilling his promises.

*Ideas taken from material presented by the Rev. John Timmer, Woodlawn Christian Reformed Church, Grand Rapids, Michigan.

But Abraham was not a completely trusting man. On two occasions he used the sexual power of his wife to ensure his safety. The first instance of this was in Egypt:

> As he was about to enter Egypt, he said to his wife Sarai, "I know what a beautiful woman you are. When the Egyptians see you, they will say. 'This is his wife.' Then they will kill me but will let you live. Say you are my sister, so that I will be treated well for your sake and my life will be spared because of you" (Gen. 12:11-13). He knew that he was offering his wife as a prostitute (of sorts). The Egyptians behaved as Abraham expected and took Sarai to the Pharaoh's house. Because of her, Pharaoh gave Abraham "sheep and cattle, male and female donkeys, menservants and maidservants, and camels" (v. 16). He gained his wealth by the power of his wife's beauty.

Abraham used a simple but effective technique to protect and enrich his life simultaneously. Unfortunately for the Pharaoh, Abraham's way was not God's. The Egyptian ruler and his household became quite ill because of Sarai; it didn't take Pharaoh long to figure out who was the cause. He expelled Abraham and his wife from Egypt. Later, the patriarch used the same technique with Abimelech (it worked once, right?). Rather than trusting God's power, Abraham trusted in the power of his wife's beauty and sexual attraction to keep him alive. God rescued his servant and saved the life of the man who might have unwittingly committed a great wrong. For whatever reason, we are not told that God punished Abraham. But we know from the context that the Lord did not approve of Abraham's behavior.

Abraham was not the last patriarch to succumb to using power. Isaac, too, lied about the identity of Rebekah. Later, he was caught between his sons Esau and Jacob, who were each struggling for power. Jacob, God's choice, lied and cheated to receive what he would have been given without his machinations. We are all familiar with Jacob's treachery, prodded by his doting mother Rebekah.

Jacob's sons followed the family pattern. Joseph provoked jealousy and hatred in his ten older brothers by bragging about how he would have power over them. Even Jacob was not pleased when Joseph told him that he, too, would bow down to him. God tempered Joseph's immature nature through the trials he suffered—being sold into slavery in Egypt, being falsely accused of sexual misconduct and thrown into prison, and being forgotten by the man he had helped and encouraged there. Through it all, Joseph learned much about temporal and spiritual power.

By the time that the Pharaoh made Joseph second in command in Egypt, Joseph was prepared. He now used his power for the good of the country and for Pharaoh, not for himself. He enriched his master, not himself. He saved his family and provided good land for them, not for himself. His example shows us that it is possible to rise to power without resorting to the tricks used by his ancestors or, later, his descendants. He also shows us that power, however rare, need not corrupt those who have it. Joseph was protected from this danger by his knowledge that he never really owned the power he wielded. He saw it for what it was— authority loaned to him for a time.

Most of us quickly forget where our power comes from. It is too easy to think, ''I earned this by my hard work or intelligence or instincts.'' It is too easy to think ourselves fine fellows indeed. When we have reached that point, we belong to power.

After Joseph, the story of Israel is one long, miserable failure in dealing with power. Moses was not immune to the temptations and abuses of power. In his anger and frustration, he murdered an Egyptian; his position at court might have made him unafraid of reprisals. But he had assumed too much. Not even his fellow Hebrews appreciated his efforts. ''Who made you ruler and judge over us?'' one of them asked Moses (Exod. 2:14). The man wanted to know from whom Moses received his power.

Eventually, God gave Moses the authority to rule the Hebrews, and for the most part he used it well. The exceptions, though, cost him dearly: The Lord forbade him to enter the Promised Land.

The situation with Moses became a recurring pattern for the leaders and people of Israel. A succession of victories made them confident in themselves and ambitious for more power, and they used many techniques to obtain it. Some of Israel's rulers bowed to false gods, thinking that the power of those gods would accrue to them. Other leaders, such as Solomon, used sexual power (political marriages) and wealth to secure their (and Israel's) position. The Israelites continually walked a narrow line between familiarity with the nations around them and the separation God intended them to maintain. Too often they fell into enemy territory. Then God would send prophets or priests to convict them of their wrongdoing. For a while the Israelites would walk as they should, but the seductions of power always overcame them.

David and Saul and Jonathan are another interesting study in power. Saul could not understand his son, Jonathan, who did not care about the throne of Israel. Saul also hated David because he had usurped his power and the potential power of Jonathan. David threatened Saul; he threatened the establishment. And what made it even more difficult to take was the fact that Saul had brought it on himself by giving David a chance to be a hero. (The man who wins in battle often finds himself in power.) Saul misused his power by trying to kill David. Subsequently, David also misused his power when he took Bathsheba and then sent Bathsheba's husband to his death.

The writings of the prophets sustain this theme: It is sinful and foolish to pursue power. Isaiah, in talking about the king of Babylon, provides an excellent description of the fate of those who fall from power—and it can happen to anyone:

> They will all respond,
>   they will say to you,
> "You also have become weak, as we are;
>   you have become like us."
> All your pomp has been brought down to the grave,
>   along with the noise of your harps;
> maggots are spread out beneath you
>   and worms cover you.
> How you have fallen from heaven,
>   O morning star, son of the dawn!
> You have been cast down to the earth,
>   you who once laid low the nations! (Isa. 14:10-12).

The taunt against Babylon continues for several more verses in much the same harsh poetic language. Maggots and worms are bad enough, but the worst thing Isaiah could say about a once-powerful ruler was that he had " become weak, as we are." The implication is clear; the pursuit of power stems from a desire to be unlike the rest of the 'earth.

Not only do the prophets recognize the fruitlessness of striving for power, but they stress that any attempts to gain it are worthless unless God ordains it or allows it. The prophets, the psalmists, and the writer of Proverbs repeat this theme. For example, Psalm 127 says, "Unless the Lord builds the house, its builders labor in vain. Unless the Lord watches over the city, the watchmen stand guard in vain." In Psalm 33, we read that the might of kings, the strength of soldiers, the superiority of weaponry is of no value to the wicked—except as the Lord allows.

To the Jewish people, it may have seemed that the Lord had allowed the wicked to flourish and reach exorbitant heights of power by the time of Jesus' birth. They had since the Exile, and before, been suffering under foreign domination.

During the intertestamental period this resulted in the Maccabean revolt. The goal was to recreate the Jewish nation. Eventually Israel again regained its independence, this time ruled by the Hasmoneans, no strangers to the techniques of power. Under that dynasty the offices of high priest and king were consolidated in one person—a shrewd move. But Pompey and the Romans took over the nation in 63 B.C. during another civil war, this time between Hyrcanus II and Aristobulus II. Once Rome controlled Palestine, it had no desire to relinquish it.

In 47 B.C., Caesar appointed Herod the Great, an Arab, to rule the region. He took the title King of the Jews by consent of Rome; he ruled by placating the power of Rome. He was an ambitious man who knew how to gain power—by currying the favor of those with more power than he. Although the Jews enjoyed some religious freedom under Herod the Great, it was not enough. Herod improved the lot of the Jews, but at their expense, with heavy taxes to pay for his building programs. Wealthy Jews who benefited by his rule were not entirely disturbed by it or by Roman domination. The poor of Palestine, however, fiercely hated the Romans.

Roman rule was increasingly more intolerable. The political

situation after Herod's death did not improve, for the three-part division of the kingdom failed to work. Archelaus ruled Idumaea, Judea, and Samaria; Herod Antipas, Perea and Galilee; and Philip Batanea, Trachonitis and Auranitis. Antipas began as a popular ruler, but he couldn't control the unrest in Galilee. Rome removed him and appointed a procurator—four came and went between A.D. 6 and A.D. 26, when Pontius Pilate took over. Yet, Pilate's governorship was ill-fated almost from the beginning. He had little understanding of or sensitivity toward Judaism; invariably he made the wrong choices in dealing with the people. Early in his administration he infuriated the populace by displaying banners of the Emperor Tiberius. On another occasion, he tried to build a needed twenty-five-mile aqueduct with money from the temple treasury. The people did not care that the project was a valuable one.

These and other events caused a ground swell of feeling that now if ever the Messiah should come. The spate of false messiahs had merely whetted the Jewish longing for the real one. They wanted a powerful military and religious leader to overthrow the Romans and reestablish the throne of Israel. Into this atmosphere, Jesus was born.

Jesus was uninterested in the politics of his day. He did not want power or its gifts. To use the language of psychology, Jesus knew who he was and what his role was to be. He already had a name, Son of God, Son of Man. He was unconcerned with acquiring his own space or striving for authority. The rest of us have to struggle with this problem of identity and self-worth, which is where we are most vulnerable to power. But Jesus is not only our Savior; he is our example. Paul tells us that we are to be like him. As his followers we receive his name, or at least a small part of it. He is the Son of God; we become children of God. He was resurrected; so will we be.

If we are to imitate our Lord, we must first look closely at the way he lived and at what he said.

Jesus shows no desire for possessions, nor does he recommend that his followers become acquisitive. When he sends the seventy-two ahead of him to preach, he says, "Do not take a purse or bag or sandals" (Luke 10:4). This passage follows the difficult one on the cost of discipleship. Everyone and everything, says Christ, has a place—except the Son of Man.

Contrary to the advice of those who know how to acquire and use power, Jesus demands unself-serving behavior. There is no room in the gospel for climbing the rungs of the ladder of power. In the Sermon on the Plain, Jesus pushes righteousness to its limits:

> But I tell you who hear me: Love your enemies, do good to those who hate you, bless those who curse you, pray for those who mistreat you. If someone strikes you on one cheek, turn to him the other also. If someone takes your cloak, do not stop him from taking your tunic. Give to everyone who asks you, and if anyone takes what belongs to you, do not demand it back (Luke 6:27–30).

We have read those words innumerable times and have heard sermon after sermon preached on them. But few of us live them. They don't seem practical in a twentieth-century professional world. (One of the many books on management contains a discussion of a Christian manager who was attempting to live out Christ's words in his business dealings. The authors conclude that he wasn't a very successful manager—and also not particularly happy about his position.)

We must balance these words of Jesus by his teaching on stewardship. Several of his parables deal with the subject—the parable of the ten minas (pounds), the parable of the fig tree, the parable of the shrewd manager. To be a good manager you may not be able to turn the other cheek, or you may not be able to allow someone to steal from you. You owe the person you work for as much as you owe the person who works for you. Can you allow someone to legally embezzle from the company by not giving a full day's work for a full day's pay? It may be something as simple as that. And it is your responsibility of stewardship in that case not to forgive the offense, but to punish the offender.

There is no denying that there are some knotty teachings in the Gospels. The parable of the shrewd manager (Luke 16:1–13) is just such a passage. In this story, Jesus seems to commend the use of a form of power—wealth—while in the rest of his teachings he speaks against it. Certainly, one of the quarrels he had with the Pharisees dealt with this issue. In this strange story, a rich man believes that his manager has been embezzling from him—or at least has been so sloppy in his work that the waste was corroding the employer's wealth. So, he orders the manager to prepare the books for an audit and fires him. The manager knows he will need another job, but doesn't know where he will find one. As his last official act, he meets with his boss's creditors and reduces their debts. The boss commends his dishonest manager for his shrewd business dealings (though we are not told whether the owner rehired his manager). Christ concludes with a strange statement: "I tell you, use worldly wealth to gain friends for yourselves, so that when it is gone, you will be welcomed into eternal dwellings" (Luke 16:9). Yet, a few verses later, Luke records Jesus' famous words about trying to serve two masters —"You cannot serve both God and Money."

This passage presents us with alternatives—God or money. Jesus is saying that we can choose to be shrewd, like the dishonest manager, which certainly had its rewards, or we can choose to be wise and faithful to God, which may not have rewards on earth but will ultimately provide us with eternal dwellings (but only when we are stripped of our possessions). The dishonest manager successfully saved his own hide by shrewdly serving money, but he lost his soul.

God, then, detests what men value. He condemns those who strive for fame or fortune. Jesus rejects the use of power as we have come to understand it. When, after feeding the five thousand, he realizes that the people "intended to come and make him king by force," he goes into the hills alone (John 6:15). Another time, before the Feast of Tabernacles, his brothers recommend that he leave Galilee for Judea, where he would have a wider audience: "No one who wants to become a public figure acts in secret. Since you are doing these things, show yourself to the world" (John 7:4). Jesus isn't interested. Even his brothers completely misunderstand his role.

Christ rebukes his disciples on a number of occasions for their concern with which one of them was the most important and powerful. At the Last Supper, the final Passover that Jesus celebrates with his twelve intimates, the men argue about which one of them will be called the greatest. Jesus explains that such thinking is unworthy of them; that is the way unbelievers behave.

> But you are not to be like that. Instead, the greatest among you should be like the youngest, and the one who rules like the one who serves. For who is greater, the one who is at the table or the one who serves? Is it not the one who is at the table? But I am among you as one who serves (Luke 22:26, 27).

No follower of Christ should think about his status, position, or place. Service is to be the mark of a Christian. Jesus washes his disciples' feet—in those days the ultimate symbol of a servant.

During the last hours of his life, Jesus also shows a complete disregard for the normal instincts of power-driven personalities. To most of us it matters that people know who and what we are—especially that we are right (the corollary being that others are wrong). We cannot bear to lose; winning is everything. Jesus is so very right, his accusers so very wrong; yet he dies without defending himself.

Although Jesus was unconcerned about power, everyone around him seemed to be—and he was caught in the middle of it. (To a lesser degree many of us are caught in a daily web of power, often through no fault of our own.) The Jewish leaders, particularly the chief priests, had an uneasy truce with the Roman governor. They feared that Jesus, because of his following among the people, was a threat to their power. They were anxious about the Roman reaction to his presence. Annas and Caiaphas used the arguments of expediency and power to convince Pilate to crucify Jesus. Pilate, himself no stranger to trouble or the hunger for power, wanted to protect his position.

The tenuous freedom that the Jewish people received from Rome—the freedom to practice their religion—was being threatened. The Pharisees and the other aristocrats of Palestine strived to keep the balance between the Roman procurator and the people. Their power and that of the chief priests depended on good relationships with the Roman-appointed governor.

Then along came Jesus, who appeared to them to be a political as well as a religious hindrance. Thus the Jewish leaders had a double reason for wanting Jesus dead. He broke their laws; he had a large following among the people; he threatened the peace at Passover. For two (or three) years, Jesus had been teaching what the leaders considered rebellious principles, not only about their laws but about the practical way the world works. No power-driven person likes to think of himself as obvious. He doesn't want those things pointed out—certainly not while he is entertaining friends or potential allies over a meal. And certainly not by a poor rabbi he had invited to join the party in a condescending show of magnanimous behavior. (Could it have been a social coup for someone to invite the mysterious and controversial Jesus to dine? Wouldn't it be today?)

Luke records Jesus' warning to his disciples about these leaders:

> Beware of the teachers of the law. They like to walk around in flowing robes and love to be greeted in the marketplace and have the most important seats in the synagogues and the places of honor at banquets. They devour widows' houses and for a show make lengthy prayers. Such men will be punished most severely (20:46).

Jesus' warning is a description of someone searching for power. Rich clothing. Recognition. Special treatment. Seats of honor. Courted and catered to at parties. After that description, no one should have any difficulty spotting such a person. About the only thing that Jesus leaves out is the habit of name-dropping—but then, that's a kind of vicarious power, or power-by-association.

Not only does Jesus say those things to his followers, he says them directly to the people he condemns—the scribes, Pharisees, and lawyers. He insults them in the marketplace, in the synagogue, and in their homes. Jesus even ignored the ancient traditions of proper behavior by a guest—traditions still practiced today, traditions fundamental to society. Jesus accepted hospitality and then used the occasion to upbraid his host. One such incident is recorded in Luke 11:37–53. Because Jesus had not washed his hands before dinner, which was part of the law, the Pharisee, his host, was surprised. Try reading the passage as if for the first time. Or imagine a guest of yours saying those things to you. No one would tolerate it. Jesus accused his host of being full of greed and wickedness, of neglecting justice and the love of God. He called the guests foolish lovers of the most important seats in the synagogues who rapaciously longed for the greetings in the marketplace. He leaves out no one around that table. Is it any wonder that the scribes and Pharisees opposed him ''fiercely''?

On another occasion, Jesus criticized the way the guests at a dinner were behaving. ''When you give a luncheon or a dinner,'' he said, ''do not invite your friends, your brothers or relatives, or your rich neighbors; if you do, they may invite you back and so you will be repaid'' (Luke 14:12). He also urged people not to seek the best seats in the house but rather to humble themselves. Although Jesus was immune to power, he was well aware of the strength of its call.

That Jesus was immune we know from the account of his temptation in the wilderness; Satan tempted him with power. Obviously, the second temptation—offering to give Jesus all the kingdoms of the world, ''all the authority and splendor''—is a direct temptation to grasp power. The other two temptations are for Jesus to show his power—to create food and to overcome death. They are an appeal to use the power Satan knew Jesus already possessed. Jesus rejected all three.*

Jesus had a ministry of powerlessness. The verse in Zechariah, ''not by might, nor by power, but by my Spirit, says the Lord Almighty'' (4:6) certainly applies to the life of Christ. He took as his purpose the words from Isaiah 61:1–2. His message in the Beatitudes was aimed at the powerless: the poor, the sorrowful, the meek, the pure, the peacemakers, and the persecuted eventually will receive great reward. Each of these categories is an-

---

*Capon sees the temptation as evidence of two distinct views of power. Satan says to Jesus, look at the good you could do with power. Jesus replies that with all that power, good would sour.

tithetical to the pursuit of power. A certain demeanor—what would be called hutzpah in some parts of the country—cannot live within a sorrowful or meek person. The qualities of mercy, purity, and peace-loving crowd out the drive for power.

Jesus used sheep as the symbol for his people.* What are sheep like? First, they are harmless. They are defenseless. They are powerless. Without the protection of the shepherd, sheep would be in constant danger from the wolves who encircle the sheep pens, wolves waiting to devour them. Jesus Christ says that he sends us out into the world as *sheep,* not as lions or foxes or wolves. That is how powerless we are to be.

But we no longer seem comfortable with the image of sheep. So, we've (figuratively, though in some cases literally), put ourselves in the hands of an image-maker. Sheep don't win many prizes, we say to ourselves, so let's have someone remake our image into something more successful. So we try to become lions or wolves. Because the power of the wolf over the sheep is so evident, we think we can best protect the other sheep, and perhaps convert a few wolves, if we become wolves, too. Then, we say to ourselves, once we become the power of the wolf pack, we can ensure that those poor sheep we left behind will be protected. Why, they won't even need a shepherd any more.

But what we don't realize—or won't admit to ourselves—is that no wolf will let himself be ruled by someone inauthentically wolf. In other words, a wolf knows his own kind; if a sheep succeeds in becoming a wolf leader that means he has become wolf inside and out. His instincts, not just his image, will have changed. And he will want to kill those sheep.

Jesus knew this. He also knew where power came from. Even human power or political power can be had only as God allows. When Jesus stood before him, Pilate said, "Do you refuse to speak to me? Don't you realize I have power either to free you or to crucify you?" Jesus answered, "You would have no power over me if it were not given to you from above" (John 19:10–11).

There is a power, however, of which Jesus approves; this is the

*For some of these ideas about sheep and wolves, I am indebted to the Rev. John Timmer.

power he promises to give his disciples. Jesus gives his followers a spiritual power to overcome evil, to resist temptation, to serve him—a power to defeat power. There is no personal merit to be gained from it. It comes from God and can be removed by God.

9.

9.
PAUL AND POWER

Most Christians think that when you are in Washington you can cop out on your Christian convictions, but I think the real temptation is power, not immorality.

—Mark Hatfield

The apostle Paul will always be an enigmatic character. No one today quite agrees as to who he was or what he was like; we do not know enough about him to satisfy our curiosity. But everyone agrees that he made the Christian church. His personality dominates the New Testament epistles, almost more than does Christ's in the Gospels. Certainly, Peter's character is not felt as strongly, despite his position in the Jerusalem church.

But why mention Paul's personality? What does that have to do with our subject? Because we can learn much about power from what Paul says directly and indirectly about it and from what we learn of Paul in his writings.

If we try to read the Epistles and the Book of Acts as if for the first time, and look at them the way a literary critic would study a play or poem, we discover some interesting things about Paul. A literary critic looks at a piece of writing two ways—in its historical context and in isolation—at the material itself, as a living thing that can tell us much about what it means without resorting to anything outside itself. This approach is particularly appropriate and helpful in studying letters, in this case the letters of the apostle Paul to his fellow believers. Good letters reveal the nature of the person writing them, and Paul wrote good letters.*

Understanding Paul will help us better understand what happened at the Jerusalem council, at Corinth, and at Galatia. It will also help us better understand the role that power played in the development of the early church. Paul by his own admission, and supported by Luke's history, was a man of no half measures. When he committed himself to a cause, he did so unreservedly. As Saul, he did not spare himself in his persecution of what appeared to be a new wing within Judaism—to Saul a heretical wing. He traveled to search and destroy the new Christians. His only goal in life seems to have been to save Judaism from these Christians. Paul was definitely a company man. He was tireless, fearless, relentless. He was unshakably convinced that he was right and that Peter, and Stephen, and the rest of those renegade Jews were wrong. In any way he could, he intended to impose his will on them.

This is a picture of a man who had no little dealing with power. Later, after his conversion, Paul wrote to many churches regarding the source of his past power: he was a student of Gamaliel, a Pharisee of the Pharisees, a Roman citizen, all of which within Judaism and Roman culture gave him power. He was used to influence, accustomed to being obeyed. Saul was a force to be reckoned with, which the new Christians knew. That was why they feared treachery when he told them about his conversion on the road to Damascus. Saul would have gone to any lengths to impose his view of the truth onto the Jewish Christians. The high priest had given him the power to do so, and he intended to use it.

Then this man met Christ on the road to Damascus, and God reversed his direction and changed his goals forever, as symbolized by his name change. But Paul still had the same background, education, and upbringing. He did not lose his Roman citizenship or forget all he knew. He even appealed to the sources of his past power to convince people that he was sincerely con-

*We will be using the New International Version. We must trust that the translators have put into English the essential meaning of the letters from the original languages, which is all one can ever hope when reading any translation, whether it be the Bible or a book by Alexander Solzhenitsyn.

verted. Would a man like that, he asked, give it all up *unless* he
had truly changed? Later, he appealed to his Roman citizenship
when his life was threatened, something, he was later told, that
worked to his detriment. He used his knowledge of the Old Testament in his preaching. And he still was the person who was
accustomed to exercising influence. The cause had changed, his
motives had changed, but he still knew how to wield power.

   We do not like to think of Paul as less than perfect, but the fact
is that he was not perfect. He was not another savior. Sometimes
he was wrong. Sometimes he was unloving. Sometimes he was
harsh and disagreeable. Sometimes he did not practice what he
preached. Sometimes his enormous ego got in the way, as we
shall see in some of his letters. We should not be dismayed when
we look at Paul realistically and see faults, any more than we
should be dismayed by an honest look at the patriarchs or David
or some of the prophets.

   Paul is definitely a study in power—both positively and nega-
tively. The fact that Paul was an apostle, received inspiration
from God, and *was* ultimately right in his teachings is beside the
point for this discussion. What we are considering is *the way* Paul
was affected by his use of power—by what we might almost call
his desire for power. If most of us in some small way, or large,
are not immune to it, surely we cannot claim that a man of Paul's
stature was. He was not. But God used him in a way that he might
not have been able to use a lesser man. Paul's confidence, ego,
and ability were large enough for the task God had at hand. And in
God's hands Paul's weaknesses became strengths, became chan-
neled in the right direction, as Paul himself many times admitted.

   Of the many situations involving Paul that occurred in the early
church, two are most instructive: the conflict between the Jewish
and Gentile Christians, and the conflict among believers in
Corinth. These two incidents clearly show the influence of
power, and show how leaders and followers were anxious for
preeminence.

Certainly the theological issues that divided these early Christians were real. The Jewish Christians were convinced that Gentiles had to become practicing Jews in every sense to be Christians also. Paul was equally convinced that to do that would be to dilute the message of the gospel and to belittle Christ's atonement for the whole world. Peter seems to have been caught in the middle—attempting to maintain his ties with his co-workers and his culture while at the same time encouraging Paul, whose preaching was obviously having a deep impact wherever it was heard.

The Jewish followers of Christ had a long, rich heritage. They and their forebears had been chosen by God to receive his special revelation. And, of all the Jewish nation, they had recognized that the Messiah had come. The disciples had no idea, waiting in the Upper Room for the coming of the Holy Spirit, that one day soon Gentiles—unclean and uncircumcised (unregenerate, we might say today)—would enter their fellowship and ultimately take it over. We must remember that to an observant Jew his relationship with God depended on his remaining ceremonially clean. That meant abstaining from blood, from meat sacrificed to idols, from eating or associating with Gentiles. (Remembering this makes us realize how incredible it was that Thomas would touch someone who had been buried.) Yes, Christ had come to free them from these things, and in many ways they were already free. But habit dies hard, especially religious habit born of culture. It was one thing for Jesus to let them pick grain and eat on the Sabbath. It was quite another to eat pork or ignore circumcision. They could not see all the implications of what Christ had done. Paul could.

True, they had accepted Cornelius into their fellowship. They had Peter's dream to convince them that what God had declared clean they had no right to declare unclean. Nevertheless, the Jewish leaders from Jerusalem must have believed that the situation was getting out of hand. Their hands.

The Jewish Christians decided to make it difficult for the Gentile believers to convert by requiring circumcision and obedience to the law. Without authorization from the apostles, some people traveled to certain Gentile communities to tell them these requirements. Paul and Barnabas went to Jerusalem to staighten out the matter. The debate there resulted in a compromise; no one won, yet no one lost. From what we read elsewhere in the New Testament, Paul did not intend to remain in that neither-fish-nor-fowl situation.

Some believers from the Pharisaic party insisted that following the whole law of Moses was necessary for salvation. Peter listened intently and then spoke to the group, defending Paul's position—in part. ''It is my judgment, therefore, that we should not make it difficult for the Gentiles who are turning to God'' (Acts 15:19). He added that only four requirements were necessary: abstaining from food sacrificed to idols, from blood, from the meat of strangled animals, and from sexual immorality. The conference appointed Judas and Silas to travel with Paul and Barnabas and so instruct the converts. Of these four requirements, only one is still in force today; Paul questioned some of the others not too long after that.

The issue for this council was power. Which group—the conservatives, the moderates, or the liberals—would prevail over the others? Who had the votes? one might ask. A twentieth-century reporter covering this meeting would certainly have asked the question, much as a journalist would today whose beat is Capitol Hill and whose assignment is the House Ways and Means Committee. If the conservatives had won the day, the history of the early church would have been quite different.

In any debate—whether in the government, in the church, in a family, or in a business—doomsday rhetoric is the order. No matter what that administration or the issue, people on both sides believe it is a life-or-death situation. If the right decision isn't made, and, of course, each side believes that it knows the right decision, history will be irrevocably changed. The energy crisis, the budget, the particular marketing concept, the new organ or building—whatever the issue, its outcome will have cosmic effects. Certainly Paul believed this in his fight to prevail over Judaizers. In his case, he was right.

The report in Acts downplays the difference between Paul and the others. (Luke doesn't hesitate, however, to inform his readers about the fight between Paul and Barnabas. "They had such a sharp disagreement that they parted company," Acts 15:39.) Paul's version of the disagreement between him and the Jerusalem Christians indicates a little more vinegar. He told the Galatians that he openly accused Peter of hypocrisy. While with Gentile Christians, Peter lived as a Gentile, said Paul. Then, perhaps fearing the good opinion of some Judaizers, Peter "began to draw back and separate himself from the Gentiles because he was afraid of those who belonged to the circumcision group" (Gal. 2:12). As if that weren't bad enough, Paul continued, Peter convinced other Jews to join him, including Barnabas.

This disagreement is no small matter, and Paul was fighting with every weapon at hand. He shamed Peter publicly. He berated the Galatians in strong language. He pretended to disregard the powerful at the same time pointing to them as accepting him—thus having it both ways. He dismissed "those who seemed to be important—whatever they were makes no difference to me; God does not judge by external appearance" (Gal. 2:6). He waved them aside as having no influence on his ministry. But then he cited those reputed pillars—James, Peter, and John—as having given him the right hand of fellowship. These are techniques to power. Paul was maneuvering to convince the Galatians that he should be listened to—he, Paul, who received his message only from God and was also accepted by the apostles who had traveled with Jesus. And here, as elsewhere, he assured his readers that he was not seeking power; obviously if he were, he implied, he wouldn't have all this trouble.

Paul didn't mince words. He admitted that before his conversion he was a violent man. Yet some of his letters contain violent language. Paul's disagreements with other believers were undoubtedly sharp at times. It was practical as well as providential that Paul's ministry was to the Gentiles and Peter's to the Jews. Paul warned the Galatians not to be misled in this issue, not to follow another's understanding. He accused his enemies, interestingly enough, of wanting power over the Galatians. "Those people are zealous to win you over, but for no good. What they want is to alienate you from us, so that you may be zealous for them'' (Gal. 4:17). In other words, Paul was accusing the others of wanting to gain followers by theft. His view of these "judaizers" was harsh: "As for those agitators, I wish they would go the whole way and emasculate themselves!" (Gal. 5:12). The entire letter is filled with such rhetoric. Should someone today write of fellow believers in such language, the Christian community would rise up against him.

Peter, of course, was not the enemy to the Gentile ministry that Paul seems to indicate in Galatians. The Galatians material must be read in the context of Paul's comments at the Jerusalem council. But, nevertheless, these disagreements do show the tension of people striving for supremacy within the early church.

Factionalism. Seeking for power. A desire to sway believers to one view or another. A fresh reading of the New Testament shows that rather than being the exception, this was the rule, as, if we are honest, it is still the rule today. If we continue in our honesty, we must admit that disputes really stem from a desire of one person or group to control others. It is too convenient to hide behind slogans of doctrinal purity, righteousness, or truth. The method of defense belies the reason given for the defense. (Remember, Paul did not know he was writing Scripture. For him, as for all Jews, Scripture had already been given.)

The worst reported case of factionalism in the New Testament is found in 1 Corinthians. Paul had learned about the power struggle going on among the believers in Corinth and wrote to stop it. But in doing so, he revealed himself prey to this struggle. This issue was more than who followed whom; it was who would have the upper hand by having the most followers and whose interpretation of this new religion, Christianity, would prevail. We tend to forget when reading the New Testament that "theology" and "doctrine" as we think of them today did not exist. Paul and Peter and Apollos and Cephas were applying their skill in the interpretation of the law or in Hellenic thought to the development of Christianity. It should not surprise us, then, that there were disagreements and that Paul was quite often found in the midst of them. Rather we should be surprised that there weren't more disputes.

Paul began by pleading with the Corinthians for unity. Who cares, he said, whether you were converted under the preaching of Apollos, Cephas, or me? The important fact is your conversion. But the desire for first place is too strong for these new believers, and they must think of "their man" as the most important. Note that some were even claiming that they followed no one but Christ (1 Cor. 1:12). Although Paul couldn't speak for the others, he could defend himself. He, after all, didn't really baptize that many people, so it was not his fault that this division had arisen. This time Paul was not putting himself forward.

Paul was a strange combination of humility and pride. When he believed that he was right, he fought to win; but he could also discreetly remove himself from the fray. Or at least show us exactly what the fray was.

In this instance the issue was power—or power by association. Paul contrasted that with the power of Christ, a power promised to the disciples before the Ascension. Paul believed that striving for earthly power could empty the cross of Christ of its power, the nature of the one being so different from the other. But the concept and meaning of spiritual power has become a foreign language to us, so used are we to the meaning of secular power.

In chapter three, Paul returned to the subject of power when he accused the Corinthians of being "worldly." Their worldliness stemmed from nothing other than a desire for power. They were jealous of each other; they quarreled constantly; they were still worried about who was premier. "Are you not acting like mere men?" Paul asked. The basic tendency of humankind, he implied is to desire power.

The Corinthians bore all the signs. They wanted a special place, special recognition, a name unique among believers; they wanted importance. They were name-droppers. (Don't we judge others by the people they know? Don't some Christians seem a little more intensely Christian—the way some reds can be more red, or some blues more blue, than other reds or blues? Add a little endorsement-by-association to someone and his Christian colors seem a little more alive.) Paul scored a direct hit when he

asked, "For who makes you different from anyone else?" (4:7).
Notice that he asks *who* and not what. Knowing a person, or
persons, cannot make us different.

Paul was interested in both kinds of power: in fighting secular
power and in explaining spiritual power. He knew that power
meant influence, and he was afraid that the wrong people would
hold sway. Look at the warning he issued about his impending
trip to Corinth.

> Some of you have become arrogant, as if I were not coming to
> you. But I will come to you very soon, if the Lord is willing, and
> then I will find out not only how these arrogant people are talking,
> but what power they have. For the kingdom of God is not a matter
> of talk but of power (1 Cor. 4:18–20).

Talk is cheap, he said, but what is your power? Where does it
come from? Here Paul used the word *power* twice, both times
meaning spiritual power, though someone who understood the
word differently might think he was referring to influence,
strength, persuasiveness, the ability to rule others. Could these
people show that they had been given spiritual power? Paul had
the credentials, the authority, to ask these questions.

In 2 Corinthians he admitted that *he* fought against his tendency toward the wrong kind of power, his conceit stemming
from a desire to be first among many. There was a good reason
why God refused to remove Paul's thorn in the flesh. Paul said it
was to keep him "from becoming conceited." In other places, he
said it kept him "powerless," if not in reality, at least psychologically in his own mind. Paul needed to be reminded, over and
over again, that left to himself, his god would be power—as it
perhaps was, ultimately, before his conversion. God, who is
Power, does not compete with the lesser gods. God told Paul that
only through powerlessness could his power be manifest in him;
only through Paul's weakness could God's strength exist in his
body.

Paul, like any other person, wanted some credit, some sign of appreciation from the people he loved. And his love for the Corinthian church can be read in every line of his two letters. Perhaps he felt that it was not returned as it ought to have been. There are lots of ways to say, "please love me." In these two letters Paul used many of them: pain, hurt, anger, frustration, disappointment, and bruised pride.

Second Corinthians 11, when read in this light, is an anguishing document. Paul said he robbed other churches "by receiving support from them so as to serve you" (v. 8). He boasted and bragged and could not stop because of his love for them. He had a cutthroat commitment to "keep on doing what I am doing in order to cut the ground from under those who want an opportunity to be considered equal with us in the things they boast about" (v. 12). He could brook no equal and accused those who were trying to usurp his place of falsehood. Yet he matched them claim for claim.

They were Hebrews? So was he. They were Israelites? The same. Abraham's descendants? Again. "Are they servants of Christ? (I am out of my mind to talk like this.) I am more. I have worked much harder, been in prison more frequently, been flogged more severely, and been exposed to death again and again" (v. 23). Paul at this point was a man driven, by anguish and hurt pride, to brag about his power as a minister of the gospel. It is not fair, he seems to cry. Not fair to reject me. My leadership has not made you inferior, because I am not inferior (this statement comes later in chapter 12). Haven't I just proven it to you? His pain also shows through in his sarcasm. "How were you inferior to the other churches, except that I was never a burden to you?" he asks. And then, bitingly, "Forgive me this wrong!" (v. 12:13). Such deeply human reactions. I've been too good to you. I've given you the best that I've had. I've sacrificed myself. I've worn out my body in your behalf. I have fought for power *for you,* and now you turn your back on me.

How often have we said to someone, "I did it for you. For you." Or heard someone say it to us? A husband who works long hours leaving a wife lonely. "I did it for you." A mother who pushes her daughter into popularity. "I did it for you."

But did we? No. We did it for ourselves. We wanted to be rich or famous or beautiful. Powerful. All for ourselves. And no love or gratitude can come to a person who so acts. The sacrifice is worthless.

But God can redeem worthlessness and mixed motivation and make it valuable. Paul knew this. He knew that God would humble him to exalt himself and preserve the work.

Paul's two letters to the Corinthian church show us several things. They reveal an extraordinary man—a man of passion and intellect, a man of will and discipline, a man committed to Christ no matter what the cost. They reveal a man who knew he was proud and loved first place. It was no accident that Paul's metaphor of the race and the prize occurred in Corinthians. Paul loved power and knew its danger. But he also knew another kind of power and willingly risked all for its sake. In many ways, we see ourselves here: Paul, an Everyman.

The Corinthian letters also provide a description of ourselves. Believers who quarreled, fought, were jealous, were subject to fits of anger, gossiped, loved arrogance and disorder. But _this_ was the church Paul loved so desperately that he revealed himself to it completely. He made himself vulnerable, to use a contemporary psychological term. It was a church that had much in common with him. Its weaknesses were his weaknesses, its strengths, his strengths. He called himself their father, and he knew what he was saying.

The patriarchs, judges, priests, kings, prophets of the Old Testament, and apostles of the New, Paul included, were imperfect men who struggled against becoming children of the lesser god, power, to become the children of the greater God of Power. We learn from Scripture what each kind of power is, what it demands, and what happens to those who choose one or the other.

10.

10.
THE PRINCIPLES
OF TRUE POWER

*God can know no holding back, no selfishness,
no fear of loss of power, no threat of diminished
existence.*

—James Ruse, from an essay in
Power and the Word of God

Any novelist or English teacher will tell you that it's easier to describe wickedness than goodness. Wicked Becky Sharp, the major character in William Thackeray's *Vanity Fair*, is far more interesting than Amelia, her moral counterpart. Without the contrast, would we be able to recognize goodness when we meet it?

This is also true when it comes to defining and describing the power God gives. Now, we could just list the fruit of the Spirit and perhaps feel confident that we know the meaning of true power. But, fruit can be seen, held, tasted, smelled, touched. What does love look like? How does joy smell or peace taste? If they are the results of true power, and they undoubtedly are, how do they become the results? How do we know them?

Scripture provides the principles by which we can develop a theology of power. When acted upon, they grow the elusive fruit of the Spirit. The two sections of Scripture that most fully describe true power are the account of Creation in Genesis 1 and the gospel report of the Last Supper. These two passages can help us understand the properties of power: power that creates, redeems, transforms, heals, unifies, strengthens, feeds, serves, resurrects,

makes whole, and communicates. Christians are not called to
worship power, but we are commanded to allow power, God's
power, which has all those characteristics, to flow through us. Of
course, that can only be done by utterly ridding ourselves of any
taint of the other. We unfortunate creatures can't do this entirely,
of course, because we can merely approximate what we ought to
be. We are reasonable facsimilies, if you will, but we should
strive to be the best reasonable facsimilies we can.

But first, following Thackeray's example, let us contrast the
two kinds of power. The lesser god, power, promises addition; it
wants us to believe it is reality, when all the time it is the negation
of reality. Although we may think we are eating bountifully, we
nevertheless starve.

The opposite of negation is creation. *And God said. And God
made. And God created.* These are sentences from Genesis 1.
The God of Power makes and makes and makes. He brings order
out of disorder. He brings life out of death. He brings beauty
where there was ugliness. He brings joy from sorrow, laughter
from tears. He is creation itself. We have only to look around us
to see the evidence and bounty of his creative power. Color,
texture, shape, sight, sound. He has provided us with infinite
combinations in nature; he has given us ability to recreate from
his ingredients. Through God's Power, we are able to imitate
Christ in his creating power. We can make ideas, we can create
beauty, we can make or mend relationships, which are probably
the most satisfying evidence of the creative power at work in us.

In looking at the story of creation, we find summarized all that
we need to know about *the characteristics of true power.* In the
first chapter of Genesis, we read of the greatness of true creative
power. God was joyous in his making of animate and inanimate
objects, all of which would willingly serve and praise him—the
just response in view of his creativity. *God creates order out of
chaos,* which is the first characteristic of true power. He brings
into being structure, pattern, shape, and form where none
existed. He does so with discipline and economy. We don't usually think of God as disciplined or economical, but certainly those
are characteristics revealed in Genesis 1. He has a plan—creation
of the earth. He understands what needs to be done and how it

needs to be done—the proper sequence, the logic of creating, the wonder of it all. And he does it economically, succinctly. He says and acts no more than is necessary to achieve his end—power focused and properly used. He speaks. He names. Life comes into being. God wastes nothing. Everything has a place and a meaning. Earth has no extras. Luxury would have been unknown before the fall; to have luxury you must also have want.

By the means in which God creates, we see the perfect example for us. First he establishes the principle. Order first—the proper atmosphere in which power can operate. Yet he doesn't so much create order out of chaos as transform chaos into order, and by so doing redeems chaos. Out of God's creative act, the first and foremost characteristic of his power, we see two other characteristics of true power, _transformation_ and _redemption_. Christ's ministry showed this power in action. He used everything on earth that he and his father used in creating the earth. Creation can never be seen apart from redemption and transformation.

Next God separates light from dark, creating the concepts lightness and darkness. Again, the abstract, or theological, first and later the physical manifestation—the sun, moon, stars, day, night. This pattern recurs throughout Scripture. And in the life of Christ we see it fully revealed. The progression is marvelous.

Jesus speaks theologically of the principles of true power in the Sermon on the Mount. Then his parables take the progression another step—principles in storytelling, during which the people could hear how someone, maybe someone just like themselves, acted on the principles of true power that Jesus espoused.

But how wonderfully did Jesus himself practice those principles and reveal them in his actions. He created a whole person when he accepted the sinful woman's tears. She was transformed and redeemed by his creative power. She and the many others who were restored and healed were then in contact with true power. They became conduits who were told to pass this true power on, to live within it and through it. The lesser god wants his followers to hug their power to themselves; if others are as powerful as we, what's the point of having power? It's only good as long as it puts us above and beyond our fellow human beings. The true power of the greater God demands that it be shared. To hug it to ourselves—and say definitely "It's mine! It belongs to me!"—is to lose it for the power of the lesser god.

After the principles are in place, the results of the principles come into being—the seas, the sky, the animals, the inhabitants of the principles of order and light and dark. The creatures now have a place that is ready to live in, a place that will sponsor growth and health and strength. A place of true power, until another act broke the pattern. Until Adam and Eve wanted to stop living by true power and grasped the power of the lesser god.

Although we occupy a broken planet, Christians have, or should have, the resources to create, redeem, and transform brokenness into wholeness, sickness into health. God puts these properties at our disposal for his use and our eager obedience. We are to be like the leper who understood the order of things—thankfulness first, restoration into society second, witness, third.

We do not want to be thankful. We do not want to *need* to be thankful. We do not want to admit that we *must* be thankful. It implies a certain worthlessness on our part, an affront to our pride and individuality. God gives us something out of the ordinary, something we didn't earn, perhaps something outside our own power to earn, though we surely don't like to admit that, which is why there's a crowd in the corridors of power. But we must be thankful. Just as the first order of creation was to be thankful and praise God for life, we must be thankful. We must discipline ourselves to it, and, paradoxically, out of that discipline, hard as the yoke on a team of oxen, comes a freedom to true power. When this freedom of power exists, nothing is blocking the pure and proper flow of power *through* us and out into the world.

The Book of James speaks urgently of the results of true power, its visible evidence on earth. Not many of us enjoy reading it, since it smacks of a works salvation and not a faith salvation. This issue is unnecessarily divisive and hints of the lesser god's desire to bend our understanding of true power to his view. James says no more than what Christ lived. He also fleshes out the fruit of the Spirit that Paul listed. What does love look like? How do we experience it? Emotionally? Intellectually? Or physically? What did love look like as practiced by Jesus? He fed people. He touched the untouchable. He healed their infirmities. He never dismissed their frailties. Finally, he ate with his enemies—that is, he accepted hospitality from them. We can recognize and admit power at work in everything but the latter. Jesus didn't suffer from the lesser god. Most of us can touch people who are less fortunate than ourselves, but not as a result of true power; rather, it is a result of the other god's impetus. We may be convinced that it would enhance our reputation, increase our name, be financially advantageous, show our humility, or, even, our power in helping someone who had not been helped before. But the one thing we cannot do is accept hospitality.

I mean hospitality in its fullest sense. Not just a meal, but a favor, help, comfort, understanding, strength. All of these are aspects of hospitality, and they are difficult enough for us to accept from those we love. But what about from those we don't love? Or those who don't love us in return? If we receive hospitality from an enemy, as Jesus received food from those he knew would ultimately crucify him, don't we have to go back to the beginning, to the principles out of which true power comes, and discipline ourselves to *thankfulness* for the hospitality? So, one evidence of true power may be our giving sacrificially. But it could just as well be our receiving sacrificially.

This principle is something that Paul perhaps had difficulty understanding. He wanted to be beholden to no one, not even the Corinthian church whom he loved. He bragged to them how he had never asked them for anything, even though it would have been legitimate. In that way, he denied them the opportunity to practice true power. He denied them the chance to give materially what they had received from him spiritually. Both giving and receiving are necessary ingredients, or aspects, of true power. Christ gave much; but he also received much by the ministrations of the women who traveled with him and the disciples. God himself is not immune from this. He must receive the praises of the people to whom he gives his power and goodness. These two exist in balance when true power is present.

The difficulty in many relationships is that the balance is disturbed and thus the harmony disrupted. What results is an adversary atmosphere, rather than a creative, transforming, and redeeming one. This opens the door to illegitimate power; it enters and begins to operate. This is true between husbands and wives, parents and children, labor and management, employers and employees.

Look first at a traditional marital relationship. The husband supports the wife monetarily. This is a clear act of giving; he gives to her the wherewithal to eat, be sheltered, raise their children. She receives this from her husband's hands, willingly and joyfully at first, just as he gives it. But he doesn't see her gift to him: an orderly home, clean clothes, wholesome food, loving children. She joyfully gives it, but he cannot see it as a gift. Perhaps subconsciously he thinks of it as what he "pays" her to do. Or perhaps he does not know how to receive; he never learned how to discipline himself to thankfulness and gratitude. What results from this is chaos, the domain of the lesser power. The progression reverses itself. At its extreme, the wife entirely stops trying to give her gift—no cleaning, cooking, caring—and the husband then stops giving his, either literally or by niggardly and begrudgingly allowing a pittance for his wife. The relationship dies.

The same scene can be, and often is, played in the business world. The employer may not recognize the need to receive his employee's gift of good work. I've heard many managers say, "That's what we're paying him (her) for." True, in one sense. But what of the worker who consistently gives more than he or she is paid for? Who does it willingly and joyfully, even sacrificially? The employer, if he or she wants true power to control, must be disciplined for gratitude. The employee, too, must accept the gratitude in the same spirit. "I don't believe in thanking people for doing their jobs" is an ungrateful attitude and will in boomerang fashion come back to maim any manager who holds it. Eventually the worker who gives more than he is paid for will cease his efforts. And the employee who only gives what he's paid for, no more nor less (and that often begrudgingly), may soon do even less than that. The adversary attitude—the ungracious, ungrateful outlook—will reproduce itself, eventually to the dismay and perhaps failure of the employer and employee. If he cannot accept hospitality, he will soon find an inhospitable atmosphere around him. And the lesser god will have won.

Creativity suffocates in an inhospitable atmosphere. When you wonder which power is at work in a person or situation, look first for any signs of creation. If you see, instead, destruction and disunity, you know which one's at work. Of course, only someone completely twisted by the lesser power would deliberately kill or maim for the pain of it. But it is possible to see the lesser power at work in other, more subtle, ways. In relationships, for instance, whether in a family, a church, or an office. Are people being drawn closer together? Does harmony rule? Are people becoming better than they were before—more loving or thoughtful or productive? If the answers are yes, true power is at work, creating beautiful relationships not possible without it. But if there is a fracture, a crack, a break, then the lesser god is present. Often, both may be there, but it takes just a little of God's power to mend the break and set the bone.

American business may be learning this lesson. Wayne Alderson, a Christian, while vice president of operations for Pitron steel company in Pittsburgh, tried to allow true power to transform the plant. He practiced both the giving and receiving aspects of this power. He showed divine creativity in his management of the plant, he injected new work rules, transformed an unwholesome atmosphere into a wholesome one, and accepted hospitality from his supposed enemies, the union shop leaders. They, in turn, learned to do the same with him. They and he had to practice the reciprocity of giving and receiving, which is the result of true power at work.

What happened amazed everyone. A faltering plant became profitable and the quality of the product increased. The men were unified, strengthened, fed, made whole. They communicated with each other and with management in a way no one believed possible. Pitron experienced resurrection, the final and great result of true power.

Unfortunately, not everyone was worshiping in the same place. Pitron was sold to people who walked the aisle of the lesser god. Alderson was fired and his creative atmosphere smothered. The resurrection was reversed; the plant died. Alderson was ahead of his time, too advanced in his understanding of the giving and receiving that results from right worship. But there are signs, perhaps borne out of economic necessity, that business and labor may take another look. It would also be good to see Christian business and labor look in the same direction (of course, they should have been there ahead of secular business).

The giving and receiving of true power will help us see life as a whole. The principles that operate in corporate life also operate in the personal and spiritual life. We make so much more difficulty for ourselves by compartmentalizing life. We call one part of living "secular" and another "sacred." This encourages us to use words sloppily and to infect them with meanings they should not have. But we can see the wholeness of life when we recognize that a person cannot worship the god power during his working hours without taking that worship and its results with him when he goes home or enters his church.

When God created the earth, there was nothing secular to be found. Life by its very nature was sacred, and thus humanity's acts in and for nature had to be sacred as well. In making humanity in his image, God allowed them to partake (to have a share in, but not own) of his power—to participate with him in creation, redemption, and transformation. Human creatures were given authority to nurture other creatures by feeding them, strengthening them, and communing with them. They had authority to renew and replenish the earth and thus be unified with it, all creatures together praising their Maker morning and evening.

God also said, "subdue and rule." Many believe that is an encouragement to power. But remember our definition of true power. Does God intend that we should force our fellow creatures into modes and patterns that are unnatural for them, to use them for our purposes, to usurp their place in God's order? Does he mean for us to manipulate them for our good or some imagined

good or for our desires? Or did God intend that we should be
caretakers of the earth, to take care of our fellow creatures and
serve them? Shouldn't we rule (use our authority) by promoting
a creative atmosphere of reciprocity? Unfortunately, we read
his command with the full infection of the lesser god in our
bloodstream.

At the heart of this is the idea of communion. God communed
with his creation, calling it good. The creation communed with
itself as Adam and Eve named every living thing. To complete
the circle, the creation communed once again with its Creator.
This is the natural rhythm that exists where true power controls:
God speaks to us; we speak to each other; we speak communally
to him. This pattern is inherent in the Last Supper—Communion
—the pattern and rhythm that emerges at the end of the Gospels
and controls the balance of the New Testament. It should control
us today. In this event, true power is physically and spiritually
manifest.

Christ took two basic elements of human existence, bread and
wine, and imbued them with the power of his presence—his
creative, sacrificial act that redeems and transforms us. His bread
and wine feed and strengthen us as he serves them to us. They
heal our souls and renew our hearts. They bring us into union
with our Creator in the only way possible since we sinned in
Eden.

The bread is the symbol of his power and his body. Yet it is
somehow so much more than a symbol. His body is our bread—
our source of food and strength, the vehicle through which we
receive the true power that will enable us to create and shape and
redeem our fellow creatures. His blood is our wine—quenching
our thirst, enriching our lives, hardening our muscles, deepening
our red blood cells. It is the vehicle through which we receive the
true power to give our blood for our fellow creatures.

And that is the point of the Last Supper. Our Lord gave his
body and blood for us, and to us, so that we can go and do
likewise. We are made in his image—his creative, redemptive,
transforming image. We are given his body and blood, the ele-

ments of his power that can create, redeem, and transform humankind. To show our thankfulness, we pass his power among as many as we can. This is the proper progression: the manifestation of his power—the gift; the disciplined gratitude for that gift—the receiving; the sharing of the power—the giving away and worship; and the godly receiving of the power back to himself. This true Power is not ours to keep, but only ours to accept and quickly give to someone else. We don't own it; we have no right to it. It is a grant gladly given from its Source. And only for a time.

What was the historical result of the giving of the bread and wine, the body and blood? It was the Resurrection. Life. Chaos transformed. Principles practiced. Negation fed into fatness.

There is no easier way to discern which power predominates than to look for the resurrection in a relationship, in a situation, in an organization. If you see people in transformation, you see his true power. If you see lives resurrected and service given and received, you see true power. But where the body suffers from fractures, pain, infection, division, silence, hunger, or dissatisfaction, know that the power of the lesser god is near.

Yet also know that a small bite of bread and a single sip of wine can quiet the stomach and assuage our thirst.

11.

11.
THE END
OF POWER

*Power has become the supreme value, the only
one that is universally recognized.*
                —Paul Tournier, *The Violence Within*

Power and work have an undeniable relationship. My concern
with power originated with my career. Others have had the same
experience. Paul Tournier, for example, believes "that the fasci-
nation of power may well play an important part in the doctor's
choice of his career." We have seen that many Christian business
people do not think it possible to work effectively without the
help of power. We have heard from several Christian writers who
assume that power can legitimately be sought and used, provided
our reasons are right. Many Christian professional women want
to help other women achieve power; they believe that without it a
profession is not possible. These women point to the ways men
have operated—the I-scratch-your-back-you-scratch-mine syndrome, the network, the traditional male areas where decisions
are made—and have said, "We must make our own equiva-
lents." There is hardly a section of our society today that is not
touched with the longing for power.

As difficult as it might be to do, Christians must say no to
power, individually and corporately. A decision for power is
antithetical to a desire for God. We must reject the reasoning that

says without power we cannot achieve; without power we cannot work. Power may help for awhile, but ultimately it will sidetrack, discourage, and neutralize us. Rather than working, we will spend our time and energy trying to protect our power. And this, if we understand the true nature of work, is unacceptable.

Work is a sacred act, a calling, a vocation. There is no unimportant work in God's eyes. He consecrated the act and nature of work by his Incarnation. Every insect, every tree, every animal was equally important to him. We might call God the first manufacturer. He showed us the beauty and joy of work, and he insisted that Adam and Eve share in it.

Even before the Fall, the first couple had tasks for which they were responsible. The result of the Fall was not that they had to work, but that the work would seem to them difficult, or painful, or unpleasant. Human creatures have been struggling ever since to surmount that agony and bring back to work something of the holiness and pleasure it had in the Garden of Eden.

Because God is a God of work who understands its meaning, he showed us great mercy when we were cursed and expelled from the Garden. He could have taken work from us entirely. He could have sent us into the world with *nothing to do*. Think of that. A lifetime stretched out desert-like, filled with—nothing. No comforting, challenging oases on the horizon. No small mountains to climb, streams to cross, bridges to build. No possibility, ever, of achievement or of failure. Sands of nothingness. The horror of it is almost incomprehensible.

Ask a recently retired person. Television and radio pummel us with the tragedy of still-capable retired men and women set aside from society. The English writer Barbara Pym brilliantly captures the transformation from worker to retiree in *Quartet in Autumn*. With no reason to exert herself, one of the main characters quietly slides into dishabille, madness, and death. Her reason to live had disappeared. Many people lose their anchor to reality without work. Their personalities can quite literally undergo massive change when placed on the edge of that desert of nothing to do.

The punishment of nothing to do would have held no possibility of redemption, of grace. But the requirement of work, no matter how hard its appearance, meant that our connection with our Maker would be maintained. God gave us the possibility of reenacting in our own small, humble, perhaps menial ways, his work during creation. He also gave us the need to imitate him in resting from our work. Then, he began the process of bringing us back into unity with him through work sanctified and dedicated to him. In sending his son, he completed it.

Even after redemption, God continues to use work to teach us, lead us, perfect us. We also must not overlook the work of the Cross—a phrase we have heard so often that we miss its meaning. It is not merely a theological phrase that sums up the Atonement. Rather, it means quite literally what it says. Christ worked—and hard—when he died on the cross. It was his vocation, the work for which God had prepared him. Christ's labor on the cross may not have been easily done, but it was lovingly done. It was also work done from a totally powerless position. There was no other way it could have been accomplished.

Work is part of God's nature, of Christ's, of the Holy Spirit's. It is an inexorable part of life. It is not something to distract us from our relationship to God. Rather, it is the thing that can bring us closer to him. James recognized something of this when he insisted that our faith should show in our work. This may be why so many people are tempted into some kind of "works" religion. There is something so basic about our need to work that we can mistake work as the end in itself and fail to see it as a symbol of our link with God. Work in Scripture is a paradox—important on its own and yet totally unimportant. We need work. We need it to feel useful, important, meaningful. We have a need to be something more than parasites in the bowels of society. We want to participate in replenishing the resources of life. We do so through work. Some people would say work makes us human. Rather, it makes us godly.

That's all well and good for those who have meaningful avenues of work, some people may say. What is and what is not "meaningful"? Is a writer's work more meaningful than a bricklayer's?

A tentmaker's more meaningful than a theologian's? A company president's more meaningful than a fisherman's? Compared to God's work, all our work is menial and insignificant; we cannot judge anyone's work here as less important than another's.

In many ways, we determine the significance of our work. How do we view what we do? Is it our vocation? Are we called to it? Do we do it to the best of our ability? Or do we look on work as something ugly, though unfortunately necessary? We may have asked God to redeem our souls, but have we asked him to redeem our minds and attitudes and our *work*? Do we think of ourselves as working for somebody, or for a company, or for ourselves? Or do we consider that we are working for God— *despite* what the work is?

Life by its very nature and definition is sacred, whether or not we choose to behave as though it is. Life is sacred. God through his son has redeemed it. So much of life is made up of work; work, too, is sacred.

Every Christian, despite his or her profession, works for God. A farmer plows for God. A secretary types for God. A student studies for God. We are responsible to him alone for how we work, for how we use our time and talents. We should not be trying to impress anyone but God. Not our neighbors, our family, our boss, our company, our enemies. No one but God.

To realize this and to act on it takes no particular mental skill. You need not try to envisage God standing over you, looking over your shoulder at what you are doing. You need not see God handing you your paycheck. But behaving as though it were true is crucial—and hard. Think about how you worked for God yesterday, or last week, or last year.

If you are like me, you probably didn't work very well. You probably spent more time not working, or pretending to work, or trying to get out of work than you did working. Or, perhaps what occupied your time and attention was what someone else was doing or not doing.

Maybe you worried whether you were being fairly treated. Perhaps you worked only to get more money or prestige or a better office. Or any number of other benefits that have a lot to do with power, but not a lot to do with work.

Yes, we're back to where we started: power. The lesser god. Little by little power is creeping in and crowding out work. Maybe we worry about why somebody else is promoted while we are overlooked. Maybe the other person doesn't deserve it; maybe we do; maybe we've decided to do something about it. We can play the game. We know the score. We aren't going to let anybody walk all over us. Why, who do they think they are, anyway? If that's the way we're thinking—or if it's a reasonable facsimile—a lot of work isn't getting done.

Perhaps you haven't reached that point yet, but you *would* like to see the head of your department replaced. Or you don't think the person in accounting is on the team. Or, maybe it's someone else who is making your job harder (or so you rationalize). The temptation could be strong to do something about it for the good of the organization, and, incidentally, for you.

Again, there's a lot of illegitimate power taking up work time.

Unless we're the president of a company and it's our job to worry about everyone else's (yet too often a president may be worrying about the chairman of the board or other board members and how to manipulate them), we should forget about other people's jobs. That's not your worry or your responsibility. Do your work to the best of your ability as if God were your boss (which, ultimately, he is). Once you get enmeshed in the nets of power, it is hard to free yourself.

The "if only" can get us entangled. If only I had someone else's job, or salary, or position. If only so-and-so weren't here, I'd have a little more freedom, a little more power. The company (the school, the church) would be a lot better off. If only they'd see things my way. If only I could get so-and-so to do things from my perspective. If only I had several staff members on *my* side. If only I could get the new principal to side with me in how to spend the money. If only . . . I could. . . . These are all if onlys to power. If we are busy intimidating the new staff member or buttering up the vice president, *that* has become our job no matter what description is filed in our personnel folder.

It can all start out so innocently. Just an attempt to expedite matters, to bring a little more efficiency into the office. Or a little sparkle, enthusiasm, excitement. We might use some subtle persuasion, some well-placed flattery—telling someone just what he wants to hear. We might ever so slightly alter what we've told one person in repeating it to another. A plea that we were misunderstood, misquoted, misinterpreted. An innocent protest, "That's not what I said" (or meant). Or we might try to convince someone that the idea was his, not ours, believing this will more effectively promote the idea. Or, we fail to give credit to the person to whom it is due. Someone may mistakenly assume that the idea was ours, when in fact it was our colleague's or subordinate's. We don't say it was ours; we just fail to correct the person's misapprehension.

These are all small matters, which in and of themselves take very little time. Yet, one small maneuver too often leads to another and another. Before we know it, our time is consumed in maneuvering. And that for which we started all this to begin with, the work, has disappeared.

But, let's be practical, we say. The world doesn't work without power. How can we get along without it? That reasoning will put us in the middle of power, not in the middle of a work for God.

A work of power can never be done to God. It is not work but only resembles it, as the hatched pods in *The Body Snatchers* resembled real human beings. Although the work of power acts in much the same way, it replaces the reality with a poor facsimile, which no one will see for what it is because everyone is functioning at facsimile level. Should someone recognize the reality, the facsimile makes certain that he will not be listened to or respected.

Power cannot tolerate reality. As Webber says, power is "the chance of an individual to make his own will, at the heart of a social relationship, triumph over all resistance, without calling into question that on which this chance rests." In other words, should we look at the basis for someone's supposed power, the power itself will be threatened.

But work, as a relational activity, will only be the beginning. Once power invades us, it invades us whether we are at work or at home. Soon all our relationships will be affected by the ties upon which power feeds. And vice versa, _which is why Christians cannot use power, and why Jesus rejected Satan's temptation to power, choosing instead the path of powerlessness. If God refuses to use power, should we try?_

Most of us live within intricate, delicate patterns of social relationships, not just at work, but at home, at church, in family. For these relationships to be fruitful, truth must be present, as well as those things that truth promotes: respect, tolerance, mutuality, inter-dependence, acceptance. It is impossible for power to exist side by side with truth. As a philosopher has written, "The politician, on the other hand, has been taught by experience that truth and power cannot live side by side, because power, being born of violence, needs the support of the lie."

What lie? All those we have been discussing. False promises of grandiose futures. People who convince others that giving away their wills is for their own good. That acting against their better judgment is for the greater good. Lies that one person or group knows what is best for another person or group. We tell these things to ourselves, to each other, to society as a whole. And it recites them back.

Theodore H. White in his biography _In Search of History_ traces his early experiences in China. There he had his first job as reporter; there a struggle for power between two fiercely independent Chinese men was occurring; there lay the heart of Henry Luce, a determined powerbroker. White's work was reporting on and understanding the nature of power in the massive Asian nation. Power there meant what came out of the muzzle of a gun. Power meant the ability to manufacture a severe famine. Power meant swaying the policy of the United States—the work and temporary authority, essentially, of only a few men. But White's work meant telling the truth about what was happening, which is when he ran into difficulty with Luce, his boss at _Time_ magazine. So, for the sake of his work, White left _Time,_ uncertain as to what would become of him. Not many of us are willing to do as he did—quit and risk failure. We'd rather give in to power for the chance of success.

Peter had such a choice the night Jesus was arrested. Yes, he feared for his life; at times power need only appeal to our most elemental emotions. But look at Peter's action another way, through the eyes of a pragmatic Westerner. What good would Peter have done Jesus by getting himself arrested, too? When he impetuously promised his leader to follow him anywhere, Peter hadn't known it might be to death. It wouldn't have helped the other disciples, either, for him to have been executed. Such as he was, with Jesus gone, wasn't he the leader? Couldn't he help keep Jesus' memory alive?

Peter saw arrest and death as failure, as recognition by society that he was a criminal, that he was wrong. Power always wants us to believe that; yet it promises the antidote while providing the poison.

Jesus, though, did not see death as failure. He did not view the choice of powerlessness as wrong. He could, though, have conceded the point and said he hadn't intended people to take him literally about the Son of God business. Then the Pharisees would have released him and he could have had many more years of influence and acceptance. But he knew that the price was greater than the cost of death. And through his powerlessness, true power was unleashed.

Most of us repeat Peter's decision and perhaps for the same reasons. We are afraid to die; we are afraid to fail. If we are going to follow God, and not the lesser god, we should be ready for the possibility, though.

It is possible to avoid power and still work. But occasionally, telling the truth, concentrating on the job, keeping our conscience clear of any urgings of power will not suffice. We may be free from the lesser god, but someone else may not be. We could become the victim of someone else's fall. Can we avoid being sacrificed? We may even be offered the chance to avoid sacrifice, if we fall into the procession and walk the aisle of power. In fact, it could be hinted that if we succumb, we will not only be saved but exalted. Or, perhaps, we think that after this once we will be left to do the work. The choice is between failure and survival.

The hardest decision may be the one that looks as if it will end something we love. White loved his work for _Time,_ but he had to leave _Time_ to rescue his work. This is the most complex paradox of all: when our choice may be in leaving our work to save our work. Wayne Alderson faced this. When another company bought out the organization he worked for, he was given a choice. He could keep his vice presidency, but only if he forsook his personnel policy of not using the lesser god, which of course was the essence of his vice presidency. What was the choice? It was between losing his job or losing his work, just as it was with White. And just as it probably has been with many other people. The glory for White and Alderson was that they recognized it. The shame for Peter was that he didn't.

Many of us who have stumbled into the temple of the lesser god have not recognized when the choice has been presented to us. We did not see the door looming in front of us; we did not feel the hard slap of the wood or the punch of the knob. We did not want to. We wanted to survive because we were afraid of dying. We wanted to avoid anything irrevocable.

Yes, work is sacred; it is the grace of God, mercifully and justly given to us. But no matter how much we love our work, no matter how convinced we are that it is what God has called us to do, no matter how much we believe that we must continue it, we cannot if it means falling at the feet of the lesser god. When it becomes a choice between staying and succumbing to power or quitting, we must quit. We cannot compromise, any more than Christ did. We must leave the situation. Go somewhere else. Take the act available to us. And if our work is God-ordained, we will not lose it. It may take a different form. It may be found in a different location. It may be found on our own, or within another organization. But we will have our work, perhaps even more exciting and fulfilling than any we expected.

Truth and power cannot exist side by side. If our work is true, power will kill it. By deciding for truth and against power, by what may seem to us like dying, we will find our life.

EPILOGUE

Since I left behind that fourteen-year-old girl, I have constantly struggled against my hunger for power, but it wasn't until a few years ago that I could even put a name to what I was fighting. It was an agonizing process. How dangerously close I was to succumbing to the lesser god came to me one Saturday afternoon.

I was writing to my mother, trying to give her an idea of what I was doing in Manhattan and how my life was changing, speeding up. In that letter, I told her what my goals were for the next year or so. I remember that, even as I wrote that I planned to double my income and take over my boss's position, I was horrified that I could write—and mean—those words. I don't know how she felt reading them; she never said. I know how I would respond if my child wrote so to me. It wasn't my desire for advancement that was so misplaced; it was some of the reasons why I wanted it. I loved my work, yes, and wanted to do a good job, certainly. But that had become secondary to what I was feeling about the people I worked for. I didn't see some of them working as hard as I; yet I knew they earned more. And I'd heard rumors that other people were claiming credit for my ideas and programs. I re-

161

sented my lack of power to do what I thought needed to be done to make the organization successful. I had decided that since I couldn't fight the way the system worked—by power—I would wholeheartedly join the fray and become part of the system. Using the system against the system to gain what I wanted. Using power.

At that point I had become convinced that "to make the real decisions, one's got to have the real power," as I quoted at the beginning of chapter two. I wanted to make the real decisions; I was even willing to accept the responsibility for them, something I had seen too many executives fail to do. Since no one ever voluntarily relinquishes power to another, I knew that I would have to take it. I watched how people played for position, listened for the unspoken rules, and waited for an opportunity. Before I knew it, power, not the responsibility, had taken first place. Looking back on this situation, I see how unconscious all this was. To myself, I denied that I was seeking power; my actions, though, were beginning to shout too clearly that something had gone awry. There was a difference between what I said I believed and how I was acting. Yet niggling at my mind was the idea that as long as my motives were right I could act for power. I was the best person for the job and God, I believed, was using me to make a bad situation better; this power stuff was all right.

Then I read Jane Trahey and remembered that letter to my mother, which even now it hurts to recall. A glimmer that something wasn't quite right became a searchlight. Yet just when I thought I had sorted out my motives and resolved the whys of my behavior, a surge of resentment or jealousy would pierce me. The more I thought about the question of power, the more I talked with friends about it, the more I realized that no matter how fine my motives, or how altruistic my desires, seeking power always and inevitably becomes the end of the search and not the means to an end. Also, the more I asked people about power, the more I realized that there were many others who struggled with this same issue.

But the road between conviction of wrongdoing and a change in behavior is long—especially if power has become a habit of being, which I now admit was true of me, and, I suspect, is true of most of us. I would like to be able to list several easy steps that I used in breaking myself of the habit. I can't. I didn't resign my position and I didn't ask for a demotion. Although I was promised a raise, I didn't press for one when the organization was faltering financially. That was a small victory—of sorts, since I didn't really need the money. I spent hours trying to decide in this too-gray area what was legitimate Christian behavior. I asked people whom I thought should know. I read. But I found few answers, for there weren't any Christian books about power.

Perhaps the most healthful thing I did was to hold spiritual spring-cleaning. I tried to be as thorough as I could in a conducive setting. I chose the beach, the brisk salt air helping me look at my behavior honestly. I asked myself why I wanted certain things. I prodded myself to answer whether success was worth the obvious mental anguish I was in and the hardening of the spirit that I believed I was in danger of.

These were not idle questions, they still aren't. Did I want to gain my whole world but lose my own soul? I knew that verse, and all the others like it, by heart. But I hadn't ever taken them to my care; nor am I alone. I had a friend who found herself in the same struggle. For months, no one saw or heard from her. I saw her at the beginning of her hibernation and was afraid for her, but she exited her winter with some life-changing solutions. I tell this story in conjunction with my own, not because we chose the same way to avoid power, but because how we came to our decisions is similar. We both in some manner withdrew—she physically, I mentally. We needed a period of spiritual silence to sort through the clutter of our lives—to discard what was ugly or unnecessary, and to keep and polish that which was beautiful.

Like polishing silver, though, it's not something that once done is done for good. One day in the Calvary Baptist bookstore, as I handed the cashier my check, she said, "So _you're_ Cheryl Forbes." She then spoke enthusiastically about how many of my articles she had read—and disagreed with. This was not the first time someone had recognized me. Although I was surprised and taken aback, I was also flattered. I realized then that I had not discarded everything I should have. I wanted to be named—as we all do—I wanted the power inherent in being named and in "earning the right" to be named. But I had forgotten who should do the naming: only God has the power to name us if we belong to him. Any other naming is done in the power of the lesser god.

Along with my recognition of this that day in the bookstore came the realization that the job of discarding and polishing is a daily necessity, because we have a way of bringing discards back into the house or accumulating other junk. No matter how difficult the process, it must be done.

In the end, of course, the choice is yours. What another Christian decides is right may not seem so to you. But if you recognize power and the different forms it can take, if you see that you may mistakenly be participating in a power structure, you need to decide whether you should continue or stop. For those who haven't begun, the question is whether to begin at all.

There will be bumps and bruises along the way; there will be some setbacks and failures. There will also be some unexpected rewards.